THE
CROSS-COUNTRY
SKIING
HANDBOOK

THE CROSS-COUNTRY SKIING HANDBOOK

A detailed instruction book on cross-country ski touring for both beginners and experts

By

Edward R. Baldwin

CHARLES SCRIBNER'S SONS

NEW YORK

Printed in the United States of America

Library of Congress Catalog Card Number: 73-2115

SBN 684-13420-9

"...to stride across soft white fields
through gray-barked trees smooth
in the quiet crisp cold
then, to plunge downwards
in the softness, arms reaching for
balance, watching that small
tip appearing, disappearing....
magic ...."

E.R.B. 1972

ACKNOWLEDGMENTS

Many have been of great assistance, but especially my father, Henry I. Baldwin, John Gallop, Lembit Joselin, Marilyn Field-Marsham, and Helen Vidal.

Photographs used in this book were obtained from the following sources:

Horst Ehricht, Kleinburg, Ontario

Robert F. George, Brattleboro. Vermont
1,2,3,9,11,14,42,55,72,96,98

George Hume, Toronto, Ontario
10

From *Veikko Hakulinen*, Kustannusosakeyhtio Otava, Helsinki, 1961
7

From *I Vilda Spak*, by S. Jernberg, A. Bonniers förlag, Stockholm, 1960
8

From *Der Skifahrer*, by Adolf Zarn and Peter Barblan, Arnold Bopp and Company, Zurich, 1922
12,29

Sport Schuster, Munich, Germany
13

From *Skilopning*, by Amundsen, H. Aschehoug & Company, Kristiania, Norway, 1922
16,17,18,19,20,21,27

Courtesy of Rottefella
26

From *The Winter Sport of Skeeing*, catalog of the T.A. Johnsen Company, Portland, Maine, 1905
30,31,32,33,34

Bass Sports Inc., USA
39

Bullaty Lomeo
90

From Sig Buchmayr Catalog of 1955-56 Season
78

From *How to Ski* by Vivien Caulfield, Charles Scribner's Sons, 1914
23

H.I. Baldwin, Hillsboro, New Hampshire
5,22,24,25

E.R. Baldwin, Toronto, Ontario
4,6,35,41,47,61,67,68,74,79,82,83,84,85,86,92,94,99

G.I. Baldwin, Canaan, New Hampshire
15,53,54,80,89

CONTENTS

PREFACE TO THE
SECOND EDITION

A year ago, when I began writing the first version of this book, only the first signs of a cross-country skiing revival were evident. Now the full "boom" is upon us as hundreds of thousands of people are experimenting with this very old sport.

In the course of the past year, I naturally encountered a new breed of cross-country skier, the complete neophyte, completely dependent on his sporting goods store for equipment; and for technique on books such as this one, the odd cross-country instructor or, most often, his own ingenuity. I have learned a great deal over the year about the problems facing people new to the sport and hope that I've improved the book for them.

One thing I discovered, and many experienced skiers who have read the book pointed this out to me, is that I am interested in, and therefore am promoting, a far broader range of cross-country skiing than the popular movement normally embraces. My interest in off-trail, deep snow skiing, and descents in particular, is quite foreign to the prepared track, "running-on-the-level" approach, which other books, and most professional organizations and ski area instructors are promoting. I have thought a lot about why cross-country skiing has taken this direction and have concluded that most people have looked to Scandinavia for the commercial development of cross-country skiing and for expertise in instruction and equipment. In Scandinavia, cross-country skiing is a national pastime and the athletic aspects are highly stressed. In Sweden, nearly 8,000 persons show up every year to run in the famed Vasa Loppet 90 kilometre race. Imagine how many other individuals are racing every week and weekend over much shorter distances! When Swedish non-competitors ski, they are quite content to tour beside the race course as spectators or bring hot tea to the competitors. Much of Sweden and Finland is quite flat terrain and naturally downhill technique has not, in consequence, been important.

Today in North America we look to these people to advise us and obviously we are given the same kind of skiing which is distinctly oriented towards racing technique with little regard for or interest in going down hills. This was brought home to me when I wrote my cousin in Sweden to obtain photographs of telemark technique and he answered that the telemark was rare in Sweden and that no photos were available!

All of this makes me more determined than ever to present cross-country skiing in its broadest context which certainly extends to off-the-packed-trail downhill technique, often through deep powder in dense woods, and usually demands more universal equipment, namely wider skis and cable bindings.

INTRODUCTION

Cross-country skiing has an unusual attribute among sports in that an unlimited number of people can take it up without bringing detriment to the sport itself or to the physical environment. Alpine (or downhill) skiing has grown to the point where virtually every mountain in snow country has been desecrated by lifts and trails and all areas are so crowded that one spends more time riding the lift and waiting in line to get on it, than actually skiing! Here in Ontario, the hills are so short that one feels like a yo-yo, racing up and down in the effort to get one's money's worth.

The whole new world of cross-country skiing awaits everyone who can enjoy the unique, somewhat paradoxical quality that it offers: an experience filled with thrills and excitement that takes place in peace and in quiet. The snow is there, the trails and woods to ski on and in are there, the equipment is simple and inexpensive, what else does one need? Cross-country skiing is an individual and family level sport; one does not *have* to congregate with thousands to enjoy it. Hopefully, more cross-country skiers will mean less pressure to build even more ski developments and the highways that are required to serve them, and perhaps fewer snowmobiles as well.

Most athletic activities which bring man into close communion with nature require stupendous physical training, stamina, and natural ability. One cannot "hang ten" surfing or "free fall" skydiving without having worked a long time at it. These are moments when man has a measure of control over his motions within an alien environment. They are, therefore, moments of great ecstasy.

Moving with great efficiency over deep snow on skis through woods, down and up hills, and over a variety of terrain can give similar pleasure because this is an environment which successfully resists almost all other invasion by humans unless they are armed with motorized vehicles or similar noxious devices.

Figure 2 *Telemark Slope*

To appreciate cross-country skiing and to be good at it, you must possess an inherent respect for efficiency and simplicity in doing things. If you possess this, it is all that you need. The rest comes easily.

This book will cover all one needs to know to enjoy the sport. The emphasis is on techniques which are useful for general touring and not particularly on the competitive aspect of the sport.

14

Figure 3 *Skiing in a Sugar Bush*

1   WHAT IS CROSS-COUNTRY SKI TOURING?

Touring is what nearly all skiing was during the thirties and earlier. Properly, it spans the wide range of activities from skiing across open countryside, to bushwhacking through woods, to mountain and glacier skiing, to cross-country ski racing over long distances. In the following pages, I will describe this variety, illustrating each kind of ski touring and the type of equipment associated with it. All of these forms of skiing can be carried out utilizing the equipment described in Chapters 3 and 4 and the techniques described in Chapter 5.

Figure 4 *"...Across Soft White Fields..."*

Figure 5 *Silent Woods and a Telemark*

16

Figure 6   *Precision Skiing among Trees*

GENERAL TRAIL AND OPEN COUNTRY TOURING

General cross-country skiing on prepared or unprepared trails or unplowed roads may be found at all conservation areas, parks, and many Alpine ski developments. Golf courses usually make fine touring areas for beginners due to the smooth ground beneath the snow. They are also great when there is very little snow. I usually look for as many hills as possible because the greatest fun is usually obtained in the descent. If your party consists of skiers of varying abilities, or adults and small children, open terrain is more desirable because the better skiers can take longer routes, the less proficient short-cuts, and everyone can come together at periodic intervals.

BUSHWHACKING

Bushwhacking is cross-country skiing in deep woods up and down hills. With some experience this can be as thrilling a form of skiing as there is. For me, its greatest appeal is that it enables one to escape the raucous snowmobile and also to practice precision skiing among the trees. No other means exist that are as fast or as graceful for crossing deep snow in steep cold woods. If you do not believe this is an alien environment, just try to travel two or three miles on foot in these conditions; no quicker way to cold and wet exhaustion has ever been presented to man or animal. Snowshoes represent a poor alternative; cumbersome to use, they weigh more than skis and do not enable one to make use of gravity when descending. In my opinion, their best application is for carrying loads in very deep soft snow when having both hands free is important.

CROSS-COUNTRY RACING

No competitive sport demands so much of the athlete in terms of endurance and stamina, with the possible exception of water polo, as cross-country racing. Nevertheless, youngsters and sixty-five year olds around the world are taking up the

Figure 7   *Veikko Hakulinen Winning the 50 km. at Holmenkollen, 1952*

sport by the thousands because it satisfies their competitive spirit while being an excellent means of conditioning, and is, most of all, fun.

For generations, the Scandinavian countries have dominated international competition, but recently they have been challenged by the Russians and Japanese. It takes generations of active support to develop top cross-country racers. The Scandinavians honor their cross-country athletes as we honor professional football and baseball players. Until North Americans provide this level of interest and support, they will always be second rate cross-country racers.

Many cross-country races are run over courses of historic interest, such as Sweden's Vasaloppet, which covers the 90 km. route from Salen to Mora in Dalarna used by King Gustaf Vasa in 1521, when he roused his countrymen to resist the expansionist ambitions of the Danes who then controlled southern Sweden. Today, this annual event early in March attracts thousands of competitors who all start simultaneously in a *geschmossel* start (see fig. 9).

19

Figure 8   *Sixten Jernberg Racing at Lahti, 1958*

Figure 9   *Geschmossel Start*

Figure 10 *The Author's Son, Benjamin, off for 2.5 km.*

I always appreciated racing cross-country during the years when I also raced downhill and slalom because it lasted longer and one split second of error would not cost the race. The nervousness that develops from hours of waiting for the start or studying a slalom course can ruin a racer's performance over those few moments that he actually competes. In cross-country, this simply never happens. You can be in a panic about your wax, or what you did not eat, or whether you went to the bathroom, but once you are out of the starting gate, you relax as you struggle to get your wind. After that, it's a breeze, even if it does not go well because your wax is poor and you wear out your arms poling. Even a fall on a hill is not the end of the world, or the race. Cross-

21

Figure 11 *Not Far from the Start*

country racing is like developing your own stride: maximizing glide, minimizing effort; it is a question of pacing yourself so as to make your techniques as effective as possible for the full duration of the considerable time that most races last.

I enjoy racing because it forces me to push myself. There are many competitions besides that with the other racers: the one with that expert you are trying to keep up with; the clock for the objective you have set yourself; each hill you want to stop running on; and whoever may be in the track in front of you when you are near the finish. The finish brings a feeling of exhilaration which makes the whole experience worthwhile whether you win, place, or do not place at all. You never lose.

Racing is usually done over 2 to 50 kilometer (1 to 31 mile) courses on ski tracks that are marked by flags and well prepared by weighted track-making machines or other skiers. When one racer overtakes another, he calls "track" and the other steps to one side. Normally, racers start at one minute intervals. On mass starts, it is extremely difficult to make progress because after the initial start on an open field or lake, all the racers descend upon a single track. For this reason, one must sprint at the beginning to reduce the number of persons to be passed.

In the Appendix, I have included descriptions of the international events and classes of competitors and a listing of some of the more popular touring races as well.

22

Figure 12   *High Mountain Touring*

MOUNTAIN AND GLACIER SKIING

Skiing above the timberline on snow fields and glaciers is one of the most thrilling forms of cross-country ski touring. It also requires the most skill and experience due to the combined hazards of weather, avalanches, crevasses, and fatigue. I only introduce it as a form of ski touring because, under early or soft snow conditions, the same equipment and techniques can be used as for the other forms of touring. It is properly the subject of another book.

Commonly today it is carried out with Alpine ski equipment modified to provide heel up-lift. This equipment greatly compromises the skier's ability to move comfortably on his skis. (see fig. 13)

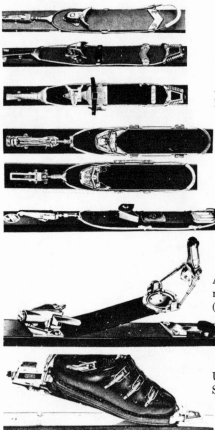

Junior Cable (approx. $18)

Regular Cable (approx. $22)

Alpine/Tour Combination (approx. $30)

Junior and Regular Touring Safety Binding (both approx. $15)

Touring Safety Cable Binding (approx. $10)

Alpine Binding with Attachment for Mountain Touring (approx. $30)

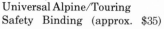

Universal Alpine/Touring Safety Binding (approx. $35)

Figure 13 *Ski Mountaineering Bindings for Alpine (Downhill) Skis*

ORIENTEERING

Orienteering is off-trail, across-terrain skiing, using a map and compass to locate checkpoints established in advance. This form of competition is very popular in Scandinavian countries, both on skis in the winter and in the summer running on one's feet. Great skill, not only in locating the checkpoints but also in choosing the fastest route to them, must be exercised. New interest in cross-country skiing in North America is already producing new interest in orienteering as well. Ski clubs interested in broadening their activities would be well advised to investigate this fascinating activity on skis.

Traditionally, orienteering has demanded bushwhacking techniques and the equipment developed for it is therefore ideal for bushwhacking. I regularly use orienteering skis, purchased for me in Sweden by my brother, that have one steel edge on the inside edge which is therefore on the inside of the downhill and weighted ski during all stemming maneuvers. I have fixed rings to these skis under the heel and can use a traditional German longthong, thus positively fixing my foot to the ski for downhill running on very hard snow conditions. With these skis, 65 mm. wide at the foot and weighing 5 lbs., one can ski any slope or terrain!

Figure 14   *Warming Up*

Figure 15 *Henry Ives Baldwin*

2 THE HISTORY OF SKI TOURING

My father, Henry Ives Baldwin, has been a cross-country skier for more than 65 years. How could I possibly write a chapter on the history of ski touring when he can do so much better? Naturally, therefore, this chapter is his work and the reader will undoubtedly note a few of his pointed comments on the direction modern skiing has taken. He has been, and is, a strong influence on my own opinions.

Skis are for transportation. Perhaps nothing more need be said. Skiing began because people wanted to travel over snow, either uphill, downhill, or on the level. Skiing requires less energy than walking or snowshoeing, where the foot has to be lifted and dragged forward through the snow. Like other means of transport, such as hiking, horseback riding, cycling or even motoring, skiing became a pastime. All of these activities originally had the objective of getting from one place to another. Competition seems to become part of any activity, no matter how prosaic or utilitarian its origin, and so it is not surprising that most people today equate skiing across country with cross-country racing. Jumping and slalom might even be considered stunts, akin to fancy diving in swimming. Downhill, the popular recreational ski sport, appears to eclipse all other

Figure 16 *Lapps at War on Skis* Olaus Magnus, 1555

forms of skiing. Is lift-riding up and sliding down the slopes the sole end of skiing? We think not. Otto Schniebs once remarked, "Skiing ist not a sport, it ist a vay of life."

THE ORIGINS OF SKIING

Obscure as the origins of skiing are, it is plain that skiing was not a sudden invention. Skiing is of great antiquity; it probably came about several thousand years ago B.C. Archaeological finds and ancient accounts suggest that one center from which skiing spread was from the Altai Mountains, near Lake Baikal in Russia. However, it is probable that it was discovered or developed independently in several places in Asia from where it spread to the Scandinavian peninsula. Fridjof Nansen, the famed Norwegian Arctic explorer, deduced this from his studies of writings and artifacts. Xenophon in 400 B.C.

Figure 17   Early "Stick Riders"

records the use of horse snowshoes, and Strabo in 20 B.C. mentions snowshoes in the Caucasus. Skis were first developed by the tribes of Siberia and Fennascandia; at first they were skins attached to frames of wood (almost elongated snowshoes), then broad slabs of wood covered with reindeer skin, and finally narrow boards. There are many references to skis in Norse sagas towards the end of the Middle Ages. Olaus Magnus (1555) wrote one of the earliest complete stories of skiing and thereafter it was frequently referred to (see fig. 16). The Swedes learned from Lapps and Finns in the Viking period.

Skiing was strictly a means of travel, for hunting and in war. This attitude did not change for over 1,000 years. Military use of skis increased in the northern countries. Skis changed from the short, broad boards with sealskins or reindeer skins permanently attached to skis of variable length. The gliding ski was 9 to 11 feet and the short ski, for pushing, was 7 to 8 feet and had a permanent reindeer skin bottom. Late in the 19th century, long skis of the same length were used. Skiing as a sport evolved from military exercises and was first practised actively in the late 18th century in Norway, only to fall mysteriously into oblivion in the first half of the 19th century. In 1831, writers recorded how rarely skis could be found, whereas earlier they had been very widespread in use.

Figure 18 *Slide Ski and Push Ski With Single Pole*

Then in the 1860's, interest revived and a central ski union was founded in 1861. Models of good ski types were distributed in an effort to restore the use of skis. The Christiania Ski Club was founded in 1877 and two years later the first Huseby, forerunner of Holmenkollen competitions, was held. At this event, Telemarken natives put everyone to shame. Stick-riding, a form of skiing in which a single pole was used as a brake (see fig. 17), was abandoned, good bindings and poles were adopted, and Norway was ready to export skiing as a sport.

Skiing was introduced to North America (as it was to the Alps) by Norwegians and was almost wholly touring until the advent of lifts. Touring, especially in the east, was what the terrain was suited for. From the Sierras and the Cascades in the western United States to New England and the Laurentians in the east, people went on ski tours. Some will maintain that this was the Golden Age of skiing in North America. Will it come again? Those who traversed the Laurentians in, say 1930, spending nights at delightful little French Canadian inns, will be hard put today to find a ski track amid the superhighways, ski lifts and pastures grown up to bush.

THE EVOLUTION OF EQUIPMENT AND TECHNIQUE

Skis

Skis for touring (or general overland transport) took different forms in different regions. The Finns, and to a great extent the Lapps, traveled over flat country which included many lakes and muskegs and so very long narrow skis served well. Being long, the skis ran straight and supported the weight over a long fore and aft span (useful in crossing thin ice, streams and bog holes). There was little need for directional control. Narrow skis offered less resistance when breaking trail. The same features characterized Swedish skis. In Norway, steep terrain led to the adoption of broader and shorter skis. (An early compromise was one long ski and one short one.) Bindings, elsewhere only a toe strap, offered more control and were developed in Norway, where jumping and slalom originated as competitive sports. When skiing was imported into the Alps and North America, chiefly by Norwegians, similar equipment became the rule.

Whether skis were long or short, broad or narrow, there was one characteristic they had in common. The upturn of the front tip was very gradual. This had two advantages. In breaking trail, the tip did not plow the snow, but slipped easily through it and over it. Secondly, in case of striking an object, such as a hidden rock or stump beneath the snow surface, or colliding into a tree, the tip did not break, but the shock was transmitted longitudinally along the length of the ski to the foot. Modern skis, designed to be used only on packed slopes, have a short abrupt up-curve in front. Cross-country racing skis also have sharp turn-ups so that they will not dig in when the back foot is lifted high in running. They, too, are intended only for cleared packed tracks. Ideally, the ski tourer should seek out unbroken snow and therefore his ski tips should curve up very gradually. Skis in Scandinavia (and Finland) were (and still are) made of birch, a native material. Early in the 20th century, or perhaps before, the Norwegians imported hickory, so popular today, from the United States. *All hickory today is still imported to Scandinavia from the U.S.* Ash was long a favorite material in Germany and Switzerland. Early skis in the U.S.A. were of maple, tulip poplar, ash and even cherry.

31

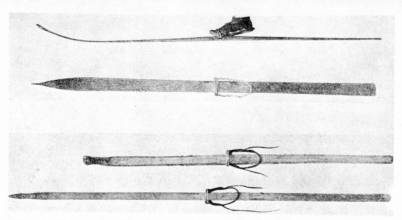

Figure 19 *Early Skis:* Telemarken skis on the top
Glide ski and push ski on the bottom

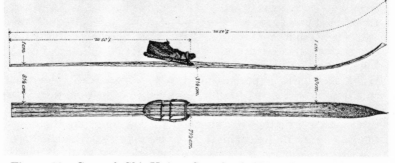

Figure 20 *Central Ski Union Standard Skis* of 1894 - Norway

Poles

Poles, or originally a single pole, were added when it was realized that arms could supplement legs and produce other advantages as well, such as braking on hills. The single long stout pole survived until the early decades of this century. The Lapps still use it, when not riding their snowmobiles. At the turn of this century, Zdarsky in Austria and Rickmers in Switzerland were pictured leaning into the slope on their stout staves. Even earlier in the 1870's, Norwegian miners in the Rocky Mountains were accomplished stick-riders. Using a rugged pole between their legs, Norwegian hunters, on long and short combination skis, relied on a sturdy staff to brake them around corners. Even Nansen in the 1880's used the single pole.

32

Figure 21 *Early Lapp Binding*

Someone decided a pole in each hand was better for balance, and even gave a better push. The earliest evidence of two pole technique was in Norway, just before the turn of the century. The Finns and Swedes had long poles as most of their poling was on the flat, pushing both poles at the same time for double poling or *stakkning*. These long poles, that reached high above the runner's head, in some cases had no wrist loops, only a stretch of leather covering a foot or more of the pole. Norwegian poles were shorter with a strong wrist loop and large rings, or baskets, as they were sometimes called, which prevented their sinking into the deep soft snow in the Norwegian forest. Swedish and Finnish disks were smaller, for more crusted and windblown conditions. Poles in the German hills and Alps tended to be much shorter than even the Norwegian ones since they were used mostly for going uphill. They were never used for assistance in turning when descending.

Boots and Bindings

Boots, like bindings, evolved from soft to hard. Lapps wore reindeer skin moccasins with a horn or upraised hook over the toe (see fig. 21), which prevented the boot from slipping out of the toe strap, but did not restrict side movement. Swedes and Finns adapted the Lapp "toe horn" to a stiff leather horn on the toe of felt boots. These had flat soles, and gave a better but still precarious contact with the ski. In order to turn, one weighted

Figure 22   *Ellesfen Shortening Clamp*
First shortening clamp around the heel operating on
a similar principle to the modern Tempo binding

the heel and pulled up against the toe strap, and thus a
step-around or step turn could be achieved even when running at
some speed. To engage the toe to the binding, the knee was bent
and the foot inserted from behind with the heel raised until the
horn could pass under the toe strap. The best Swedish and
Finnish racers used only this connection, which served them well
on relatively flat ground.

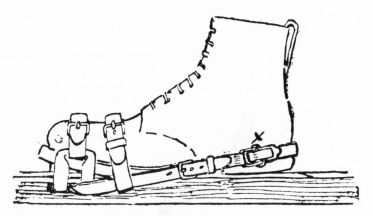

Figure 23   *The Huitfeldt Binding*

Who thought something more than a toe strap was necessary or useful, I don't know, but in 1895 Fritz Huitfeldt published a small book in which the binding that bears his name was illustrated (see fig. 23). From that time on, all the Swiss and Americans heard of was Huitfeldt bindings or at least toe irons. The latter, in original form, consisted of a flat piece of steel with a slot in the center, the width of a leather strap. The steel was about 10 inches long and 2 inches wide, and was inserted through a mortice in the center of the ski. A strap was passed through the slot in the iron and this served as a heel strap. Each end of the iron was then bent up and angled by wrenches to fit the sides of the boot sole. A toe strap was looped between the two upturned ends of the toe iron. A refinement was lining the toe irons with leather. While the toe iron was very narrow, it was a vast improvement over a toe strap alone. Next was the problem of holding the boot reasonably firm within the jaws of the toe irons. The Ellesfen Shortening Clamp (see fig. 22) accomplished this and was the forerunner of larger heel clamps such as the Bildstein, or the front-acting shortening clamps found on most cable bindings.

While the Huitfeldt binding was a great boon to Alpine ski touring, an inventive Austrian, Zdarsky, designed a radically different touring binding, the sole binding. Instead of depending on heel control by holding the front of the boot in jaws, as it were, Zdarsky in 1896, and later Colonel Bilgeri, used a steel heel receptacle on the end of a spring steel sole plate. The heel was held in this socket by a strap over the instep, and the toe was

Figure 24   *Early Sole Binding* The boot is strapped to a heavy
canvas sole which is in turn securely fastened to the
ski only at the toe

restrained only by a strap linking two eyelets. The really important part of the unit lay ahead of the toe, however. It was a cylinder, housing a stiff steel spring, whose tension could be varied. This held the sole plate down on the ski, but the heel could be lifted against the spring, and this enabled one to kneel down on the skis without any strain on the foot. One advantage was that almost any kind of footwear could be used — an asset for military purposes, as the Germans found in World War II. The only similar sole binding I have seen was one that was popular in the first decade of the 20th century. A piece of stiff sole leather was sewn in heavy canvas and one end screwed firmly on the ski under the toe or a bit behind. An over-the-instep strap held the heel as in the Bilgeri. Toe irons or straps held the toe in place, but exerted no restraining influence on heel slip as the leather sole did that. This was a mighty good binding for trips in the bush because warm leather pacs, or leather-top rubbers ("Barker boots"), could be used and consequently there was no need for a stiff shoe.

To return to the evolution of the Huitfeldt binding, during the 1920's the Marius Eriksen and Löipe bindings provided a lip under which the edge of the sole was wedged, and thus made toe straps unnecessary. Later, in the Alps during the 1930's, the Amstutz heel spring, devised by Walter Amstutz, held the heel down for Christianias yet permitted it to be raised high in the telemark. The Bildstein heel clamp was another definite improvement, being a continuous spring on the cable around the heel with a shortening clamp integral with it. Finally in the mid-thirties, the Kandahar cable binding and its variations superseded most of the other types for downhill and touring. A toe iron with a groove or lip on the side for the cable enabled the cable binding to be used as an uphill binding with free heel, or the cable could be put in the low hitch position for downhill running. New light Kandahar-type bindings of anodized aluminum are now popular in Scandinavia for touring. The Tempo binding, made in Norway, has side springs and is also an excellent touring binding.

Meanwhile, around 1910, Norwegian cross-country racers came up with a totally new binding (see fig. 25), a 100 percent toe binding, leaving the heel free. Lauritz Bergendahl, a famous racer and winner at Holmenkollen, is usually credited with the invention. Two cast bronze toe irons, hinged at the sides, had a

Figure 25 *Bergendahl Binding*
The first toe binding introduced in Norway and accountable for much of the early success of Norwegian racers

lip that pressed down on the sole edge when the jaws were drawn together by a strap. The base plate contained a number of sharp points that penetrated the shoe sole. Originally, small brass posts or studs 1/4 inch diameter entered holes bored in the shoe. The Bergendahl was the popular racing binding from about 1910 until 1930. At the first winter Olympic Games at Chamonix in 1924, Hedlund, the Swedish star, came to grief on the steep terrain, and reported when he returned to Sweden: "We shall never compete with the Norwegians until we have Bergendahl bindings." Around 1929, the Rottefella (rat-trap) and its refinements and adaptations supplanted it as a racing

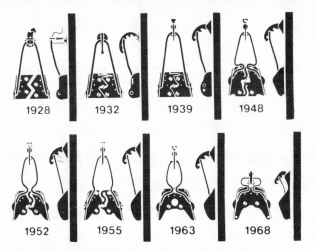

Figure 26   *The Evolution of the Rottefella Binding*

binding. Even in Norway, Bergendahl bindings were rarely used for touring. For mountainous terrain a heel-strap type binding is still preferred. Rottefella bindings are widely used now for touring on flat land (see fig. 26).

Until recent years, there was little difference between a cross-country racing boot and a jumping or touring boot. Then light low cut boots appeared for cross-country racing, and progress in downhill technique led to heavier and stiffer boots being used which were quite unsuited for touring. Further specialization led to a situation where there were no boots available that were suitable for touring. Fortunately, however, a dozen or more brands are now marketed in each Scandinavian country, and some are imported to North America.

CONCLUSION

This description of the evolution of equipment is truly sketchy and over-simplified, but is the best way to approach the history of touring. Terrain, climate, character of the people, natural resources, and the uses to which skis were put all entered into the development of ski-running. Histories of skiing have usually emphasized competition and club politics in much the same way that general histories concentrate on political events. Lunn's *History of Skiing* turns out to be mostly intrigues within ski clubs in Great Britain; and Dudley's *60 Centuries of Skiing*, hardly lives up to its title in significant

39

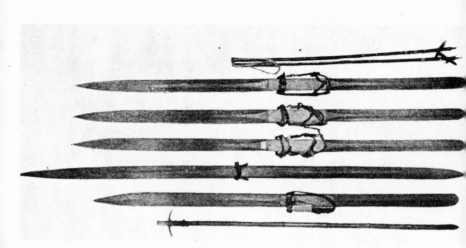

Figure 27   *Skis Used by Nansen on the Greenland Expedition*

events. Amundsen's *Skilöpning,* however, does not succumb to this temptation and while he limits his history to Norway, he covers the complete development of skiing with notable success. It is for this reason that I have principally drawn upon Amundsen's book in compiling this short account.

SKI TOURING EVENTS OF NOTE

Of all early skiers, Fridtjof Nansen made the most spectacular expeditions. His first crossings of the remote Hardangervidda and the Greenland ice cap were epic journeys during 1884 and 1888 respectively.

During the Nordenskjold Expedition to Greenland in 1883, two Lapps were sent out to reconnoitre. They returned in 57 hours, having covered 230 km.! Later, in Lapland, a race over the same distance (about 143 miles) was held; one of the same pair, Paavo Lars Tuorda, won in 21 hours 22 minutes.

Also in 1883, it is recorded that Lt. Col. Schenström skied 700 km. from the Norwegian frontier through Värmland and Dalarna in Sweden.

All of this skiing was done on unequal length push and slide skis and with a single pole.

Later in the 1890's, when two poles were introduced, annual spring "Easter Tours" for sport became common and ever since, all Scandinavian cities are traditionally empty for these holidays when everyone is off on a ski tour.

In 1888, the first skiing in Germany began when a few foresters moved there from Norway.

Sir Arthur Conan Doyle skied at Davos in Switzerland in 1895. He had learned the art in Norway.

Figure 28 *Downhill Telemark in the Pines*, Saranac Lake, New York, circa 1920, by Dr. Willard B. Soper

Early American Skiing

Rev. John L. Dyer went to Colorado in 1850, where he learned to ski from some Norwegian miners. During 1861-62 he carried mail (23 to 26 lbs. at a time, plus 5-7 lbs. of express mail) over an old Indian trail covered in 3 to 20 feet of snow. His skis were 9 to 11 feet in length and he carried a single pole.

John A. ("Snowshoe") Thompson carried mail for 20 years all winter over a similar trail from Placerville to Carson Valley, a distance of 90 miles. He used heavy oak skis weighing 25 lbs. or more and fitted only with a toe strap. His first such trip was in 1856.

Figure 29   *Double Telemark at Lilienfeld, circa 1910*

Americans Abroad

Oliver Perry-Smith, an American, competed in the first German Championship race in 1909, beating many Norwegians who had entered. He placed second over a 17 km. course. Later in the same year he won a 13.6 km. event in Czechoslovakia, also defeating Norwegians there. In 1911, he placed second in the German Championship and in 1913 won the 15 km. In that year he placed third in the Jump, was second behind Bergendahl in the Combined, and was also winner of the Saxon Championship in the Combined. In 1914 he reached the climax of his career in international competition when he won the German/Austrian Championship at Kitzbühel in both the cross-country and the Jump. In 1914 he also ran in the Holmenkollen 50 km. race and placed 14th which was quite remarkable over this distance. At Riesenbirge in 1914, he introduced the first lightweight langlauf skis and the first Bergendahl bindings. Certainly these achievements rank him as the first North American to be successful in international Nordic competition. Indeed, his successes have yet to be equalled by any North American.

Figure 30* *"The Skidor is Free to Roam Wherever His Fancy*
  Leads Him"

Figure 31* *"Skee Sails Make 'Going' Lively"*

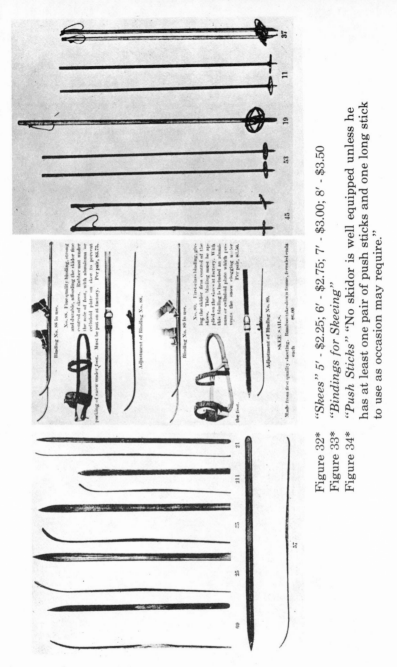

Figure 32*   *"Skees"* 5' - $2.25; 6' - $2.75; 7' - $3.00; 8' - $3.50
Figure 33*   *"Bindings for Skeeing"*
Figure 34*   *"Push Sticks"* "No skidor is well equipped unless he has at least one pair of push sticks and one long stick to use as occasion may require."

*These illustrations from a U.S. manufacturer's 1905 catalogue of skiing equipment utilized the expressions *skidor* and *skee* for skier and ski. Skis in Swedish are *skid* and he who uses them obviously a *skidor*, but *skee* remains an etymological mystery.

"A Perfection of means and a confusion of aims, seems to be our main problem...."

Albert Einstein

3   EQUIPMENT

Not many years ago, finding cross-country equipment in North America was somewhat of a challenge. Since all of our downhill or Alpine equipment before the 2nd World War generally had the capability of allowing the skier to raise his heel, we did a lot of tour skiing in those days with the same skis that we used for downhill. Actually, these combinations of reasonably lightweight Alpine skis, cable bindings, and light and flexible boots were almost ideal for mountain touring where we used sealskins for the ascent and were able to do downhill stemming turns, as well as telemarks, on the descent. For cross-country racing, we used to cut down old wooden downhill skis by ripping off about 5/8 inch of wood from each side and fitting them with a pin or toe binding which might have been sent by a relative in Sweden. I remember one outfit which consisted of ripped down skis with a pair of tennis shoes screw-fastened at the toe directly onto the ski. Actually, this was a pretty effective arrangement in those days.

Today, however, cross-country ski touring has become a big business and no less than several dozen different brands of boots, bindings and skis are available nearly everywhere. In the very recent years, large chains of department stores have gotten into the cross-country business, along with every sporting goods store. Unfortunately, the buyers for this sort of outlet have not the foggiest idea about what the sport is all about and have invariably selected, for the most part, racing equipment with the

Figure 35 *Boots*
Cross-country racing and touring styles
These racing boots (lower left) belonging to the author
Are fitted with grommets for the "Kloa" binding

result that many first-time cross-country skiers who are interested in the touring aspect of the sport have found themselves inappropriately equipped. Many retailers of equipment apparently believe that the vast majority of people either intend to race or will be skiing only on well prepared tracks. In the past this has been largely true, but I believe that skiers will increasingly seek the unbroken snow. In the following pages, I will discuss the most desirable pieces of equipment for ski touring for skiers who are anxious to handle all types of terrain and all types of snow conditions, and I shall touch on racing equipment as well.

It should be possible in most localities to completely equip oneself for ski touring for less than $75. This is buying good quality equipment, too, and it certainly represents a far cry from the high cost of good quality Alpine (downhill) ski equipment.

BOOTS (see fig. 35)

Cross-country boots range from extremely light and low cut track shoe type racing boots; through lightweight touring boots, which are only slightly higher; to a full touring boot, which is also extremely lightweight, but rises to at least the center of the ankle. The advantages of the higher boot for touring are two-fold: one's feet are apt to remain drier; and secondly, this type of boot normally comes equipped with a grooved heel for use with a cable or *Tempo* binding. (See fig. 36.)

For the complete novice, as well as the bushwhacker and mountain skier, I recommend the full touring boot. Avoid extra lining or fleece lining, which only adds to the weight of the boots and often makes them overheat and become most unpleasant when wet. Warmth is not really a critical factor in a touring boot since one normally keeps moving and is not apt to get cold. Also avoid boots with over-the-instep straps, which are only cumbersome to do up and serve no useful function. All boots should have a relatively squared-off sole, projecting approximately 3/8 inch to 1/2 inch in front of, and to the side of, the upper boot, allowing for use in a variety of bindings. I like to use a full touring boot cut just above the ankle but adaptable for use with a pin or toe binding, which requires the projecting sole. Composition rubber soles vulcanized to the upper boot are best for water tightness, but many problems have developed with some models and one should be sure the model is at least one season old and has been successful before purchasing it. Some boots come equipped with cast-in or molded-in sleeved holes for the studs on pin bindings. If the boots you select do not come thus equipped, be certain to install screw-in type brass sleeves around each of the pin holes and a metal protector plate over and in front of these.

For the tour skier who never intends to utilize the downhill techniques described elsewhere in this book, such as the telemark, or who is confined to relatively flat terrain, the light-weight touring boot with a pin binding is perhaps the best choice, even for a complete novice. This boot is only slightly heavier than a racing boot, but provides more comfort.

For the serious racer, extremely lightweight track type boots with pin bindings are a necessity.

47

All the above boots cost between $20 and $30, except for some of the best quality touring boots, which run up as high as $45. Often, however, the more expensive boots are simply lined or insulated, which is not really necessary. My favorite boots are the Kikut and Alfa, both made in Norway.

The Fit

In fitting boots, be certain that you wear the same socks that you intend to ski with and try to obtain a snug heel fit, but with ample room around the toes. An elasticized top around the boot is an excellent idea for keeping snow and water out of the boot, although I would recommend the use of snow anklets nearly all of the time.

Care

To maintain the boots, always keep them thoroughly impregnated with a *dubbin* or other preservative such as Snow Seal, which will soften the leather (therefore, inappropriate for use on Alpine ski boots). Since the soles are preferably flexible and remain flexible, it is not necessary to block touring boots when storing them.

BINDINGS (see fig. 36)

Buy your bindings at the same time as you buy your boots as the two must be entirely compatible in every way. This will be apparent to anyone examining the functional aspects of a binding.

All ski touring bindings are divided into basically two groups: the toe clamp only, or pin binding, and the cable-around-the-heel binding of which there are two varieties. The latter type, obviously, requires a boot with a grooved heel; the former requires boots with projecting soles. The cost of any of these bindings is from $5 to $8.50.

Figure 36

1. PIN BINDING: typical 3 pins-in-a-line binding, most popular for racing and for use on light weight narrow touring skis. A wide variety of types are manufactured in anodized aluminum incorporating various clamping mechanisms to hold the "bail" down. All are outgrowths of the Rottefella binding. (See fig. 26) Cost $6-9.

2. TEMPO BINDING: an extremely simple cable binding incorporating a shortening clamp within the cable itself. Made of anodized aluminum by at least two manufacturers, this binding is virtually as light as a pin and quite suitable for all kinds of cross-country skiing. The model shown allows for adjustment to fit different size boots. Some models only permit different length boots. Cost $10 - 12.

3. CABLE BINDING: this universal type of binding is made by many manufacturers in steel and aluminum. Varieties used for ski mountaineering (See fig. 13) incorporate safety release mechanisms which are not required for general cross-country and touring. Models with relatively short toe plates allow freedom of movement equal to the Tempo binding. Utilizing a front "throw" or shortening clamp, the cable can be made more flexible, thus allowing use of hold-down hooks at any interval along the ski if desired for downhill running. Infinitely adjustable, these bindings are ideally suited for growing children and for adults who ski very aggressively. Cost $8-16.

I recommend the cable-around-the-heel type binding to novice skiers and all skiers contemplating varied terrain touring where downhill techniques will be utilized. The cable type binding offers much more strength in resisting the torque of the foot on the ski that occurs under stemming conditions. The twisting forces are transmitted through the cable to the outside of the binding and, thus, more directly to the ski itself since the binding, when screw-fastened, is structurally integral with the ski. In the lighter pin type binding, these twisting forces are applied directly to the pins themselves which are placed closer together. Probably, the pin binding, when fitted perfectly, is as good as the cable binding, but in my experience I have found it far more difficult to get a tight, wedged fit in the toe iron area, especially as only the leading edge of the sole of the boot remains stationary.

Cable Bindings

Of the cable-around-the-heel type bindings, there are basically two varieties. One is the standard cable binding with a coil spring heel piece or rubber sleeve, an adjustable front-throw or shortening clamp, and a lightweight adjustable toe iron with side cable guides. This is a *Kandahar* binding and an excellent choice in that it can be fitted with an extra pair of side-mounted cable guides or hold-downs on the ski, allowing a measure of heel hold-down when Alpine or downhill techniques must be employed. It is a good universal binding for the beginner and especially for children because it can be adjusted to fit an immense variety of ski boot sizes.

The second kind of around-the-heel cable binding is a *Tempo* binding, manufactured both in Norway and in Finland, which consists of a simple light adjustable toe iron and a rigid cable fastened to each side of the toe iron and a small shortening clamp mounted on the side of the heel. This is a very simple binding, involving no forward throw on the ski and it is also adaptable to a wide variety of boots. It is perhaps the best selection for all-around ski touring by the novice since it allows somewhat greater freedom of movement than does the Kandahar binding and still possesses sufficient strength required for such maneuvers as the telemark.

Pin Bindings

There are a large variety of pin bindings on the market, most of which have three pins projecting out of the binding that fit into holes in the sole of the boot. The skier must be very careful to position his foot properly so that when the top clamp or bail is forced down onto the boot, the pins are not pushed into the sole in the wrong place, disturbing the sleeves or damaging the sole of the boot. I believe, for this reason alone, the pin binding is inappropriate for small children. The fit of the sole of the boot within the toe iron itself in a pin binding is extremely important. Normally, the sole must be shaved somewhat with a sharp knife or a plane to fit perfectly as the toe irons in many cases are not adjustable in width, but come in narrow, medium, and wide sizes. When selecting pin bindings, make certain the size is appropriate for your boot size.

Another variation of the pin binding is the *Kloa* binding, made in Norway, which has two small wires of extremely stiff and strong stainless steel which clamp *down* through grommets placed in the projecting sole on each side. This is an extremely lightweight binding and very popular with racers.

My favorite pin binding is a Troll binding.

To Mount the Bindings

The mounting of cross-country bindings is a simple matter and is often best performed by the skier himself rather than by a ski shop or sporting goods store that might be totally unknowledgeable about the equipment they are selling. The balance point on skis varies, but it generally is quite close to the center point. The leading edge of the binding should be placed approximately 1 inch in front of the balance point so that the front of the upper of the boot, when in position, falls slightly ahead of it and the ball of the foot approximately 1-1/2 inches to 2 inches behind it. Thus, when the leg is picked straight up with the ski in the binding, the tip of the ski will droop forward at an angle of approximately 20 degrees. Drill screw-fastening holes, preferably with a tapered drill, so that the screws are as tight as possible without splitting the ski; and lubricate the mounting

51

screws with a soft ski wax before installing them. On adjustable Kandahar bindings, this makes it easy to loosen the screws when rearranging the position of the toe iron. Should a binding ever loosen on a ski, I have had reasonable success in reinserting the screw with a wooden match placed in the hole mixed with epoxy resin. However, in this event, the binding is *permanently* on the ski.

Under the heel of the boot should be fitted a rubber "pop-up", or a serrated metal and rubber pop-up combination, which will prevent ice from building up under the heel. The latter variety offers the advantage of a place to scrape snow and ice from under the boot when putting on your skis.

POLES (see fig. 37)

The best all-around poles are made of tonkin cane imported from China; they are inexpensive, strong, and light in weight. For more money, fiberglass poles are also excellent and of about the same weight. However, I have found that they shatter at extremely low temperatures when striking a tree. An even more expensive alternative is the Scott pole, made in the United States, from extremely light aircraft alloy tubing. These are virtually indestructible.

All cross-country poles should have very sharp metal tips which are curved forward to prevent them from sticking in the ice and snow when they are drawn out behind the skier. The grips are ideally made of leather or cork with an adjustable wrist-strap.

Select relatively small baskets if you are racing and only interested in minimum weight and will normally be using the pole in packed snow conditions. Use larger baskets if you do a lot of off-trail bushwhacking and deep powder skiing.

The length of the pole should come to directly under the armpits when standing on a bare floor or loosely under the armpits if standing on snow, so that the pole sticks below the level of the boots. When you are selecting a pair of poles, be certain that your wriststraps overlap in opposite directions (making a pair) if they are of the nonadjustable variety. Poles cost from $5 to $20, depending upon size and material. Caring for

Figure 37   *Poles,* from left to right:
1. Tonkin Cane 2. Fiberglass
3. Scott aluminum Poles

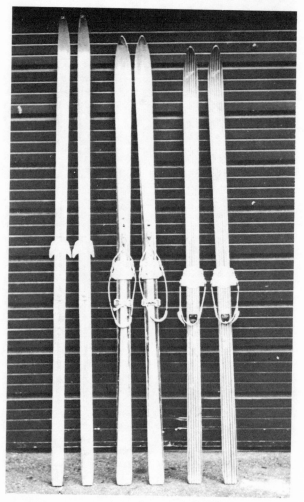

Figure 38 *The Author's Skis and Bindings*, from left to right:
1. Racing skis with Kloa bindings
2. Orienteering skis with single edges fitted with Kandahar cable bindings and extra loops for German type longthong
3. Normal touring ski fitted with Finnish Tempo binding

poles usually requires no effort, although some Snow Seal or dubbin rubbed into the straps is an excellent idea and filing the tips to keep them sharp for crossing lakes on ice, et cetera, is also a good idea. Bamboo poles should be taped at the whorls tightly with plastic tape to prevent checks, or cracks, from advancing the length of the pole. If a bamboo pole is overstrained, a check will often open up between two whorls. This can be satisfactorily repaired by drilling a 1/16 inch diameter hole at each end of the split, and placing tape over these holes and at the middle of the split. These small holes prevent the split from becoming longer.

SKIS (see fig. 38)

This is the area where uninformed store buyers have introduced many novice recreational cross-country ski tourers to inappropriate equipment by importing, and thereby encouraging the use of, only racing skis. Skis range from racing skis, which weigh less than 3-1/2 lbs. per pair and are only 50 mm. (or 2 inches) in width at the binding, to mountain touring skis which are nearly 7 lbs. per pair and up to 70 mm. in width (or wider) at the binding. For general use, I recommend a standard weight touring ski, not a lightweight one. Skis are normally made in lengths from around 190 centimeters to 220 centimeters in 5 centimeter increments. Small children's lengths are available also in the lighter type of touring ski. Most skis are constructed of lightweight birch and beech laminations, with a thin hickory sole and often an ash top plate. This is to reduce the weight to a minimum, using the heavier hickory wood only where its density is required. On the better skis, the edges are reinforced with strips of lignostone (plasticized compressed beechwood) edges.

Skis containing several dozen laminations are required to resist the tendency to warp that is present in all wooden skis. Generally, the more laminations, the better. The hickory content is minimized not because of its rumored scarcity (strictly an erroneous rumor), but because of its weight and high cost. I would not recommend purchasing skis which use softer wood, such as birch, on the sole, even though such wood holds wax far better than the dense hickory. Softwood bottoms will simply wear out very quickly in icy crust conditions.

The better manufacturers are all reinforcing the tips and tails of their skis with fiberglass sandwiched into the wood laminations. Many new wood skis with fiberglass bottoms and fully fiberglass skis as well are about to be introduced. Unfortunately, at this writing very little information on these skis is available. For waxing ease and stability, I recommend the all wood touring ski in at least the 60 mm. width.

In selecting skis, choose the length to reach the center of the hand when the feet are flat on the floor, the arm is fully extended vertically, and the palm held at a right angle to the arm. If you are heavier than average, select the next length ski to compensate. I believe that a longer ski is generally better and is essential to avoid slip-pass of the rear ski during telemarks.

When picking out your pair of skis, make certain you have a *pair* by checking the serial numbers. Place the skis on a flat surface, if possible, to determine whether they are warped or twisted and that the camber, or natural curvature of the ski, places the binding point, or middle of the ski, approximately 3/4 inch off the floor. If a dead flat floor is not available, place the heel of one ski against the heel of the other and bring the soles, or bottoms, that are immediately adjacent to the curved tip, into contact with one another to make certain they butt in perfect alignment. Small ski shops which do little business with cross-country equipment often have skis left over at the end of the season and these are not always stored in the best of conditions during the summer, with the result that by the following season they have become somewhat warped. Cross-country skis should be stored in a cool, dry place and ideally should be clamped at the tip and the tail against a dead flat surface and blocked in this position to preserve their camber. If this is impossible, block them one against the other, but be certain to check that one ski does not remove the camber from the other, which can occasionally happen.

Maintenance of the ski bottom is discussed in Chapter 6, which deals with waxing. The top surface of cross-country touring skis should be kept sanded smooth so that rough edges do not develop which can lead to splitting, and should be kept well sealed with a urethane varnish and treated with a paraffin wax so that snow does not build up on the top surfaces. Plain white paraffin wax is best for this purpose, either rubbed on from a cake and smoothed out by hand or painted on with a brush. Silicone sprays from an aerosol can also be somewhat effective for this purpose.

When placing cross-country skis on the roof rack of a car, place the tips at the rear of the car, either pointed down or up. I have seen excessive wind pressures snap the tips of lightweight racing skis when placed forward. Also, remove cables from Kandahar and Tempo bindings, or lash them with rubber bands to prevent their loss while moving.

When you come in from a tour, always place the skis against the wall in a tip-down position to prevent the water which collects on the floor from the melting snow from causing checking, or cracking, at the end of the ski.

As I have said, I recommend that the novice skier buy a standard touring type ski, not necessarily the heavier mountain type ski, but a standard weight touring ski, approximately 60 mm. wide at the binding and compatible for use with a Tempo binding. Skis of this sort run from $24 to $45 in cost and are entirely appropriate for all the downhill touring techniques described in this book.

The lightweight racing ski, on the other hand, is designed just for that purpose and can only be used on a well prepared track. I have often broken a pair by skiing out of the track at high speed into deep snow as the simple pressure of the snow snaps the tip. Because I advocate getting away from the prepared tracks, I can only recommend that racing skis are not used. The beginning skier also finds far more difficulty in balancing, both in running on the flat and in skiing downhill, with the narrow skis. Furthermore, in deep soft powder snow, the racing ski offers little buoyancy.

All touring skis are made in different flexibilities. This can be determined by squeezing the skis together with the hand and testing to see whether the pair is of hard, medium, or soft flex. A heavier person should use a stiffer ski, and lighter persons a more flexible ski. The portion of the ski between the tail or heel and the boot position should be substantially stiffer than that part between the tip and boot position. This characteristic makes the ski naturally jump forward when unweighted. Check for stiffness in this rear part of the ski and reject any ski which bends with equal ease either side of the boot position.

Lignostone is plasticized, compressed beechwood. The hardness of ski bottoms is easily determined by comparison. A very hard hickory bottom holds wax less well than the softer birch bottom. However, the hickory bottom will last far longer and provide a smooth, even glide and is preferred among racers. Lignostone edges are rarely combined with the softer wood bottoms because the wood bottom will wear away much faster than the edge, leaving them quite vulnerable to being torn off. As your technique improves, you will find that you will not wear out the edges of the skis as rapidly and generally I have found that I will break a pair of skis or split them in some other way before completely destroying the edges.

Softer birch bottom skis can be completely worn out in two or three days of skiing on glare ice. The active skier, as you can see, will undoubtedly end up owning several pairs of touring skis: stiffer plastic or hickory-bottomed skis with steel, lignostone or plastic edges for icy conditions; and more flexible birch bottom skis for deep powder conditions. Additionally, he will have racing skis, and mountain skis, not to mention his Alpine equipment and jumping equipment. It is best, when smitten with skiing to this extent, that you set aside an entire room in your basement for all this equipment; and if you have two or three children, set aside your entire basement. One saving factor is that the equipment is relatively inexpensive.

Touring skis are side-cambered to improve tracking. They usually have softer tips and slightly harder tails, allowing the tip of the ski to conform to small deviations in the track and to bite in at the tail at the end of each slide. Another advantage is that the ski tends to spring forward when suddenly unweighted due to the stiffer tail. A lot can be told about the correctness of the camber of the ski by noticing how the wax wears during use. If excessive wear occurs at the tip and tail, the ski obviously has too much camber. If the ski has too little camber, it will tend to turn up at the tail and at the tip and wear excessively under the foot. Many new developments are taking place in synthetic plastic or fiberglass construction, though proper flexibility has yet to be achieved and the difficulties of waxing, I feel, make this type of ski a poor choice for most skiers.

Figure 39 *Good Cross-Country Skiing Rucksacks*

ACCESSORIES (see fig. 39)

Aside from the waxes and wax kits described in Chapter 6, about the only accessory one need consider for ski touring is a lightweight rucksack to carry waxes, extra clothing, and food, etcetera. An extremely neat nylon one, made in Japan, that is suitable for the gear of one or two people, is available nearly everywhere; it zips into its own pocket and weighs a mere 2 oz.

Also useful in making long tours is a replacement tip for your skis because these are extremely vulnerable to being broken, especially when touring in unbroken, deep powder snow where running into concealed brush or a deep hole, or often simply the snow itself, can snap a tip off very easily. These are made in adjustable aluminum or nonadjustable plastic.

Both this rucksack and the replacement ski tip run around $3 or $4. Better rucksacks, such as the "Bergans," cost over $20.

SKI CONVERSION CHART

CM.	FT.	CM	FT.
105	3'5"	165	5'5"
110	3'7"	170	5'7"
115	3'9"	175	5'9"
120	3'11"	180	5'11"
125	4'1"	185	6'1"
130	4'3"	190	6'3"
135	4'5"	195	6'5"
140	4'7"	200	6'7"
145	4'9"	205	6'9"
150	4'11"	210	6'11"
155	5'1"	215	7'1"
160	5'3"	220	7'3"

Skis should be measured at least 10" over your head height. If you are a little on the heavy side, allow a couple of inches more in length.

Poles should be measured from the floor to between the arm pit and top of shoulder.

FAHR.	CENT.
41	5
32	0
24	-5
14	-10
5	-15
0	-17.8
-4	-20
-13	-25
-22	-30
-30	-36

BOOT CONVERSION CHART

European size	American size
28	10
29	11
30	12
31	13
32	1
33	2
34	3
35	3½
36	4½
37	5
38	6
39	6½
40	7
41	8
42	9
43	9½
44	10
45	11
46	12
47	13

Ladies: take your regular shoe size and deduct 1½ sizes from it. For example: regular size is 7 less 1½ sizes = size 5½ or size 39.

Men use regular shoe size.

BE SURE TO ALLOW ROOM FOR ONE LIGHT AND ONE HEAVY PAIR OF SOCKS

Figure 40 *Useful Conversion Tables for Equipment*

4   CLOTHING

Any kind of clothing can be and is worn for cross-country skiing. In this chapter, I will try to outline some tips on how to dress as comfortably as possible for skiing. Until recently, almost all clothing specifically designed for cross-country touring was imported from Norway or Finland, and generally consisted of lightweight cotton knickers with loose fitting parka type tops. These are now widely available from many sources and cost approximately $25 for a complete set. I have found the knicker bottoms alone, about $16, to be the most useful investment and on top I wear multiple layers of lightweight shirts and, if necessary, a windproof outer shell. Generally for touring, long wool trousers are just as good as knickers. However, some important things to remember are:

    a. Minimize the weight of all clothing where possible. This is much easier to do than one might realize. Even when the temperature is well below freezing, it is possible to wear extremely light clothing provided one keeps moving and is always reasonably near shelter in the event of a mishap, such as a broken ski.

    b. Avoid loose clothing which can catch on trees or on branches.

    c. Avoid getting your feet wet in deep snow or slushy snow conditions.

    d. In addition to weight, avoid bulky clothing which you will want to remove after you warm up, and which is difficult to store.

e. Make sure all the clothing you wear is capable of breathing so that moisture does not build up beneath it.

Often when one is touring, it is colder upon the return than when you set out as, for example, in the late afternoon hours. It is therefore wise to have a light parka or extra shirt or sweater around one's waist or in a small rucksack. Generally, unless the air is extremely cold, the clothing with which one starts the tour is the same as one would wear indoors. I quite often slip on a pair of gaiters over an old pair of corduroy trousers and simply go skiing without worrying about knee length wool socks, knickers and the like. Even with knickers, if you are skiing in soft snow conditions, gaiters or anklets are an extremely wise idea. Nearly all touring boots sold today come very low on the ankle and competition boots are extremely low, requiring anklets or wool or rubber socks if one is to remain dry.

Just as in so many other winter sports, one must exercise extreme caution when going into the woods, especially alone. Be certain that you are dressed to be out three or four times as long as you expect. On one occasion, when practicing for a fifteen kilometer race near Saranac Lake, New York, I set out at 2:00 p.m. the afternoon before the race which was a brilliantly sunny and relatively warm day, expecting to make a leisurely hour and a half tour around the course. I was dressed in the same clothing that I would have raced in as I expected to keep moving and therefore keep warm. About midway around the course, I crossed a lake where the track had been completely obliterated by the wind and, after reaching the other shore, searched for an hour and a half trying to find the trail where it entered the woods. I was unsuccessful. Eventually, I found a woods road to a nearby highway, not arriving there until after dark when the temperature had fallen to around zero and the perspiration of an afternoon's exercise had become solid ice crystals on my face and clothing. I presented such a strange apparition on the highway that the first car that came along sped past and would not stop. I was only rescued some fifteen minutes later when I stood in the middle of the highway and refused to let the next car pass. Needless to say, I was not really fit for the next day's race. My two greatest mistakes were not returning on the trail I had just skied over and not carrying extra clothing while skiing alone.

Skiing in extreme cold is entirely possible. The Firth sisters, crack Canadian stars, train at temperatures down to -40 degrees Fahrenheit at their home in Inuvik, Northwest Territories. When skiing in very cold temperatures and/or high winds, minimize the exposed portions of your body and do not be tempted to wear extra clothing which will only cause excessive perspiration. Most important, constantly check your ear lobes, nose, fingers, etc. for the whiteness which accompanies frostnip prior to frostbite. Study carefully the following chart of wind chill factors and recognize the conditions that exist when you set out and may exist before you return.

CHILL FACTORS OR EFFECTIVE TEMPERATURES AT VARIOUS WIND SPEEDS

Temperature (Fahrenheit)*

Wind Velocity (miles per hour)	35	30	25	20	15	10	5	0	-5	-10	-15	-20	-25	-30
5	33	27	21	16	12	7	1	-6	-11	-15	-20	-26	-31	-35
10	21	16	9	2	-2	-9	-15	-22	-27	-31	-38	-45	-52	-58
15	16	11	1	-6	-11	-18	-25	-33	-40	-45	-51	-60	-65	-70
20	12	3	-4	-9	-17	-24	-32	-40	-46	-52	-60	-68	-76	-81
25	7	0	-7	-15	-22	-29	-37	-45	-52	-58	-67	-75	-83	-89
30	5	-2	-11	-18	-26	-33	-41	-49	-56	-63	-70	-78	-87	-94
35	3	-4	-13	-20	-27	-35	-43	-52	-60	-67	-72	-83	-90	-98
40	1	-5	-15	-22	-29	-36	-45	-54	-62	-69	-76	-87	-94	-101

Starting at the feet, the following is a brief summary of appropriate clothing.

SOCKS

I have treated boots under the equipment chapter where I advised against an extremely tight fit. The socks you wear within these boots should be of wool, and they are usually the knee length, knicker variety. I prefer smooth, knitted, thermal socks, such as the Himalaya thermal sock, to the more ornate ribbed type woolen knee socks, which catch brambles, burrs, and snow to a greater extent.

*Based on a 3-4 mph gait in still air. (Winds over 40 have marginal effect on the chill factor, the most significant change occurring between 5 and 15 mph.)

Figure 41   *Knee Length Gaiters and Anklets*
Material which breathes is more important than
waterproofness as its purpose is primarily to keep
snow from entering the boot.

The second pair of socks is normally worn inside the knicker
socks. I prefer wearing a plain cotton "wick" type sock or a
lighter weight pair of wool socks on the inside.

GAITERS AND ANKLETS (see fig. 41)

Gaiters or anklets, as I have said previously, are essential in
soft snow or wet conditions. I wear anklets under all conditions
and full length gaiters if the snow is deep. Alternatively an old
pair of wool socks can be drawn over one's boots to provide an
effective means of keeping snow out of the boots or rubber boot
gloves can be used. However, I feel the latter are only suitable
during extremely slushy conditions and offer no improvement in
deep powder snow, when snow enters the boot from above.

When buying gaiters obtain a pair with zippers in the back so they can be put on after your boots are on. I have a pair made of rubberized nylon and, while very nice and light, they are prone to condensation on the inside and make my socks wet. The heavier, more old-fashioned canvas gaiters are better in this respect although I really believe the ideal gaiter has not yet been made. At the base of the gaiter either nylon tie-down cords, which can be tied under the instep of the boot, or a leather strap and buckle should be provided. The forward base of the gaiter should project as far as the bottom of the boot laces and be fixed with a hook so that snow cannot work its way into your boot laces. For some inexplicable reason, many gaiters are sold today which have a simple round bottom, making it impossible to pull them sufficiently far forward to cover all the boot laces.

If you choose to wear anklets for competition, or for shallow snow conditions with trousers, or for deep snow conditions with knicker socks, they should fit properly over the laces as well, but more important is a snug elastic fit around the top of the ankle and around the boot. I find a cotton type with a stitched-on elastic that fits under the instep to be the best. These need not be fitted with a zipper at the back since they can easily be slipped on before the boot.

KNICKERS, TROUSERS AND SKIRTS

Knickers are favored for cross-country skiing because of the freedom of movement which they permit. I use light cotton ones for normal weather conditions and an old pair of corduroy ones when it is extremely cold. However, most commonly I choose to wear lightweight trousers combined with knee length gaiters for all casual touring. I never wear long underwear for cross-country touring, but some people do especially if conditions are extremely cold or windy. Competitors are now using Alpine warm-up pants for warming up prior to a race, but I do not believe they have any application for cross country touring use, other than for this purpose. The very lightweight nylon wind pants as used by mountaineers are very useful to carry in one's knapsack for emergency use while touring.

Women often enjoy skiing in a skirt. For all forms of touring, except bushwhacking, it seems very appropriate. In many ways, clothing for cross-country ski touring should resemble that worn for skating.

SHIRTS AND ANORAKS

Fish-net underwear is useful in preserving an air space between all of the top clothing and your skin. When buying this type of underwear, make certain you buy it large enough as it often shrinks and it is extremely uncomfortable when tight. Over this should be worn soft, 100% cotton shirts or turtle-neck jerseys although I personally find turtle-necks hot and confining when exercising strenuously. A succession of layers of such shirts, depending upon the temperature and wind conditions, is very useful as one can shed one layer at a time; they are all light and can be rolled around one's waist or stowed in a small rucksack. A heavy flannel or wool shirt is useful for cold weather. I quite often wear a wool shirt such as this and an outer garment. Alternatively, a light nylon uncoated shell, or anorak, or a light cotton anorak can be worn. It is wise to see that this is reasonably snug fitting so that it does not to catch on branches of trees or present a large amount of resistance during heavy winds.

GLOVES

Unless the wind is strong, I tend to ski gloveless at temperatures over 20 degrees. If conditions are not too severe, light cotton work gloves are extremely comfortable but, of course, they become soaking wet if put in the snow or worn in snowy or rainy conditions. Even when wet, however, they offer substantial protection beyond the bare hand. In colder conditions, I tend to wear plain wool mittens and when it is extremely cold, I wear wool mittens inside light deerskin outer shells. Wool mittens do wear out rapidly in the palm of the hand from poling, but I have found them to be far more comfortable than any kind of ski glove. Another advantage of the wool mitten and deerskin shell combination is that if you catch your pole on a tree or shrub when bushwhacking or skiing through woods, your hand will slip out of the mitt and wrist strap more easily than it would out of gloves.

HEADGEAR

There is great difference of opinion as to what is the best type of hat. Much heat is projected from the body through the head when exercising vigorously and I, personally, perspire heavily under a wool tuque. I prefer a simpler headband or headjock of wool which is effective in keeping the ears warm, the hair out of one's eyes and sweat off one's forehead. During warmer weather, cotton "sweat bands" are very effective as well. Only under the coldest and most bitter conditions, would I wear more than a simple headband. (I have spent many hours perspiring under a balaclava at high altitudes when ski mountaineering; under these conditions, this level of protection is required because of the low chill factor present.) The great advantage of the headjock is that one can push it up on one's head to expose the ears and forehead when hot and pull it down when one is cold.

As you can see, the cost of clothing for cross-country ski touring bears no relationship whatsoever to the high cost of Alpine ski clothing.

Figure 42 *Stretching Out*

5   TECHNIQUE

GETTING STARTED

Assuming one has one's boots on the right feet, fitting the skis is quite obvious as the toe irons on all bindings slant outwards more on the outside and are more parallel to the edge of the ski on the inside, in the same way that the boots are shaped. In addition, most bindings, if Scandinavian, are marked "H" for *höger* or right, and "V" for *vänster* or left. Take care to knock the snow from the bottom of your boots before inserting them in the toe irons. With the pin type binding, be certain the pins are aligned with the holes in the boot before forcing the boot down with the top clamp or bail and putting all of your weight on it.

Once standing with skis on, move around and explore the freedom that the boots and bindings give you. Kneel on the front of your skis, pick them up horizontally by raising your foot, and watch the tip droop towards the ground.

Practice the kick turn which, for most Alpine skiers, seems unbelievably easy on cross-country skis (see figs. 46 & 47).

Jump straight up and down in place and note how the light equipment makes it possible to gain considerable height. Now put on the poles as shown in figure 43. Jump now and discover that by transferring weight to the poles, one can achieve even more height.

Figure 43 *How to Grasp the Ski Pole*

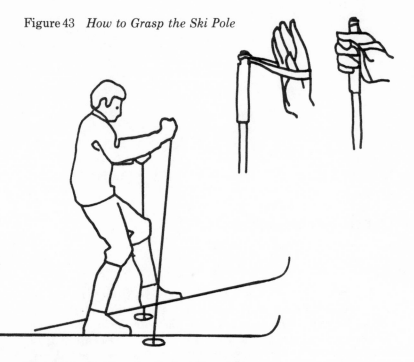

Figure 44 *Getting the Feel of Your Skis*

From the relaxed standing position, practice simple step-around turns (see fig. 45) without attempting to slide. Practice until you can change direction quickly in this way without tangling the skis, which to the Alpine skier may seem very loose and somewhat uncontrollable. Concentrate on coordinating the movement of poles and skis, keeping the poles approximately a foot away from each ski. Practice the step-around turn backwards, moving the tail of the ski out first instead of the toe. Just as the gymkhana driver must exert consummate skill to maneuver his car quickly, even at very slow speed, so the cross-country skier reveals his general level of proficiency just by the way he *stands* on his skis. Learn to be relaxed and 100% in control at all times. Learn to be able to move quickly, to change direction quickly.

The basic in-place maneuvers, then, are as follows:

Figure 45 *Stepping Around in Place*
1. Lift one ski.
2. Move it to one side.
3. Follow it with the other.

The Kick Turn (see figs. 46 & 47)

The kick turn is a fundamental maneuver for changing direction while standing either on level ground or on a very steep slope, perpendicular to the *fall line*. (The fall line is the shortest line directly down the hill.) In the latter situation on a narrow trail, it is often the *only* means of continuing down the hill, short of sideslipping down or removing the skis and walking.

To make the turn, bring either ski (if on the level), or the downhill ski (if on a slope), sharply forward and up so that the tail of the ski is placed in the snow near the tip of the opposite ski or at least half way between that tip and the boot. The ski should then be almost vertical and may be rotated around the body and replaced on the snow, facing in the opposite direction to the other

2. Swing it around the body twisting in place.

1. Raise one ski near to the vertical.

3. Place on the snow in the opposite direction.

4. Bring the other ski around beside it.

Figure 46 *The Kick Turn*

ski. The other ski is then picked up easily and crossed over the heel of the first ski and placed alongside it, thus completing the 180 degrees change of direction. Maintain your balance throughout this whole maneuver by relying on your poles. Be certain to plant them firmly and not to move skis and both poles simultaneously. Obviously, one pole must be moved with each ski movement to avoid a conflict, but the other pole should be firmly planted at these times. Some edging of the weighted ski, especially when on a hill, will be necessary to prevent the skier from sliding sideways in the very awkward position of having both skis pointing in opposite directions!

When executing the kick turn on *very* steep slopes, the downhill ski is generally moved first so that when being rotated it does not interfere with the slope itself. This also enables the skier to face outwards, bracing himself securely on his poles. Each skier develops his own preference in this regard. The kick turn is an essential maneuver to master because it can get you out of many difficult situations and allow you to proceed with a series of very flat traverses on any slope, under complete control.

Figure 47 *The Kick Turn Is the Least Awkward Means of Changing Direction while Standing Still*

Figure 48   *Very Smooth Going*

The Step Turn (see fig. 45)

The basic step-around maneuver can be practiced in place, both forward and backwards, as I have mentioned. This is simply moving alternate skis, one at a time, gradually changing direction. While standing still on the level, it is most quickly done in a backwards direction by moving the tail of each ski in succession. Simply reverse all of the motions indicated in figure 45. Great speed can be obtained by using a hopping motion from one ski to another so quickly that both skis are practically moved together. Just practice moving them as quickly as you can and you will discover this for yourself. Later, when learning to sidestep, you will discover how useful this maneuver is.

Obviously though, the step turn while sliding must be done by picking up the tips of the skis, not the tails, and so it is important to practice this while standing still. First assume a position as if about to sit in a chair and lift the unweighted tips one at a time, pivoting them on their tails. While sliding, it is important that this be done in a rhythmical way and so try to maintain a uniform and smooth sequence.

Basically, when standing on cross-country skis, try to exploit the freedom they provide. Sit on a fence post or log, kick the tip of one ski behind you and turn around while standing on one ski and examine your wax. In doing these simple things, you will develop the balance and control over your skis that becomes so important once you start moving on them.

ON THE LEVEL

After practicing the in-place maneuvers, move out in a normal walk on the level, sliding your skis with each step. It is best as a beginner to stay in a broken track (ideally about 7 inches between the skis) that has been left by other skiers or prepared by a weighted track-making machine dragged by a snowmobile. This will prevent you from crossing your skis initially, causing loss of balance, or from allowing your poles to sink in too deeply, which can have the same effect.

Concentrate on transferring your weight from one ski to the other in a rhythmical way and maintaining your body fully erect. Gradually increase your stride, forcing the forward leg out to form a sharp angle at the knee and bringing maximum inertia to the sliding ski. I concentrate on this during nearly all running or striding technique as it seems so simple; the more you are able to make your sliding ski slide, the stronger your *kick* is becoming. The application of poles should be secondary to developing this balance and rhythm. Once you have achieved this, gradually begin to apply force to your opposite pole to increase this slide. This process is called the diagonal stride and is the basis for all cross-country technique. Without an essentially smooth and effortless stride, cross-country will only be "running" and a lot of work if one is to ski any considerable distance or at any considerable speed.

The Diagonal Stride (see fig. 49)

This is the basic maneuver for cross-country skiers when they are interested in maintaining speed to cover substantial distances. Essentially, the objective is to minimize the movements of the body which cause fatigue, and to maximize the capability of the skis to slide across the snow with no effort at all. The objective is maximum glide at all times. The skier begins one stride before he has fully finished the glide remaining from the previous one. In this way, both skis are in motion across the snow at all times. This is very easy to do on a well prepared track with fast conditions, such as frozen granular snow or ice; it is somewhat more difficult to do with slow conditions.

75

1. At the beginning of the stride the weight is here on the left ski.

2. The right leg is moved forward as the skier kicks with his left leg and swings his left pole forward.

3. The skier glides on his right ski to which he transfers all of his weight raising the left ski off the snow.

4. The left ski is then swung forward with the right pole while the skier pushes downwards and backwards on his left pole.

5. The beginning of another cycle.

6. The reverse of number 2.

7. Gliding on the left ski.

Figure 49 *The Diagonal Stride*

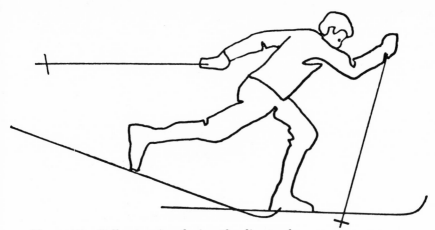

Figure 50 *Full extension during the diagonal stride is the key to proficiency.*

The basic sequence of the diagonal stride is as follows:

1. Skier, leaning forward slightly and with knees slightly bent, thrusts one leg forward along with the opposite arm and pole, planting the basket of the pole slightly ahead of, and approximately one foot away from, the leading foot. The skier is thus transferring all his weight onto that forward ski, which he rides like a scooter, while kicking off from the opposite foot and swinging the other arm behind.

2. As the slide on the forward leg carrying the skier's weight begins to diminish, just before it stops, the trailing leg is raised, allowing the trailing ski to come virtually off the ground, except for the tip.

3. Pressure is now applied to the planted pole. As the skier pushes, he draws the rear ski forward, advancing into the forward position as sharply as possible and completing the transfer of his weight onto that ski, and at the same time bringing the other pole forward to repeat the sequence. Figure 49 illustrates this process.

It is apparent that the further one pushes the forward leg forward by kicking with the rear leg, the further one must lean forward and simultaneously extend the rear arm and leg as a counterbalance. The beginner will find it very easy to topple on his face, but as a sense of balance develops, he will gradually be able to extend his reach and, therefore, the distance and duration of the glide.

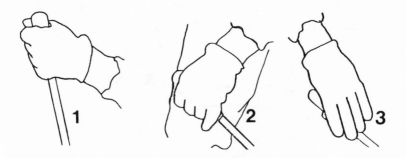

Figure 51 *Correct Hand Grasp of the Pole While Striding*
1. Firm grip while pushing
   Relaxing grip as pole travels past the body
   Fully relaxed grip as pole begins forward
   swing

Practice your stride without poles and you will realize how small the proportion provided by them is of the total power required. The poles are a timing and balancing mechanism and, while definitely contributing to a racer's total speed, have minimal effect on the speed of the tour skier. It is important to minimize the effort extended on pole maneuvers. Swing the pole deliberately forward, making use of, but not relying entirely on, its pendulum action. As each pole motion is completed, relax your grip on the pole, extending the fingers open and drawing the pole forward by the simple pressure between thumb and index finger (see fig. 51). In this way, your hand will not become stiffened and cramped.

It is important to minimize lateral body motion in your stride for the same reason. Keep your eyes on the track, approximately fifty feet ahead of you, and concentrate on keeping your head and body from bobbing up and down.

Only by paying careful attention to eliminating unnecessary movements can total body fatigue be reduced. Too much bending forward at the waist will cause difficulty in breathing; swaying from side to side will tire the back muscles; and unnecessary lateral movements of the poles will tire arm and shoulder muscles.

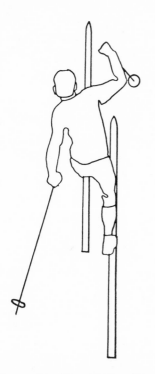

Figure 52 *The Gliding Phase of the Stride*
Top and frontal view

The essential characteristics of the diagonal stride remain whether one is skiing at racing speed or at a casual touring speed. Obviously, the successful racer must master his stride so that he can ski at faster tempos more easily. Watching world class competitors ski is a marvelous form of self-instruction. Racing against them is an incredible experience; to be struggling to maintain one's stride up an incline under conditions when one has a lot of backslip (i.e. poor wax) and hear the cry of "track" and have some Finn go by you as if you were standing still can be very disheartening. By measuring the gliding distances of skiers of varying ability, skiing at the same tempo, one will discover startling differences. Bear in mind that a matter of inches on every stride can amount to thousands of yards over a few hours. One thing you will notice when watching

Figures 53 & 54   *Easy Striding Under Ideal Conditions*

Figure 55 *Stretching Out*

world class competitors is that they maintain their forward motion, never remaining static on the forward ski. This is the hardest refinement to master and only by subtle and rhythmical forward and backward motion of the upper body is it possible.

Finding the appropriate tempo for maximizing speed under different snow conditions can only be learned by the individual skier for his own level of ability. Slow snow, resulting in a short glide, will naturally tend to increase the rhythm of one's strides, while fast snow will tempt one to hang onto the glide phase for longer, and thus slow down the rhythm.

Double Poling (see fig. 56)

Double poling is nothing more than swinging both arms forward, while in the beginning of a single stride, in order to plant both poles simultaneously and, leaning forward, drawing both feet together into a glide. The skier crouches as he extends his poles as far as possible behind him on the follow-through and, on retrieving them for the next poling action, rises and lunges forward to extend the poling distance to the maximum. Double poling is useful for providing a change of pace from the normal stride and for downhill running when one wishes to increase one's speed.

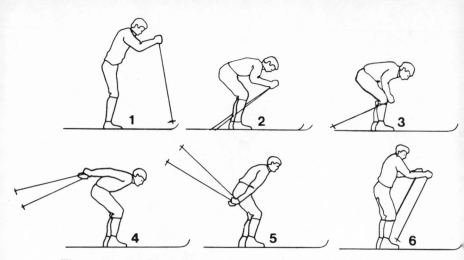

Figure 56 *Double Poling*
1. Poles are about to be set and the skier's weight transferred to them.
2. The skier bends over the poles, knees bending.
3. Pushing at maximum knee bend.
4. Follow through with poles.
5. Poles are allowed to swing forward.
6. Positioning poles for a repeat.

Any racer who has been caught with an enormous amount of backslip in his wax, and thus has ended up double poling his way across long flats will testify what an exhausting procedure this is. For short durations, however, double poling is extremely restful and can aid in catching one's breath after a strenuous hill climb or the like. It is also very useful on a track filled with many small bumps, where it is difficult to maintain the rhythm of the diagonal stride and to maintain the glide that would otherwise be lost through an interruption in this rhythm. In racing, I always start into a downhill section of the course with some brief double poling to build up speed quickly before resting in a crouch position. While touring, double poling is quite often useful when crossing a lake with a strong wind at your back under fast conditions or simply on long slight downgrades.

Figure 56 illustrates the phases of the normal double poling operation. Figure 57 illustrates this process while taking a stride simultaneously with double poling, which is nearly always the way all skiers begin the maneuver.

1. Skier has forward inertia.
2. Poles are swung forward weighting one ski for kick.
3. Kicking for glide and stretching out for maximum pole travel.

4. Planting poles and bringing legs together.
5. Weight over poles while bending knees.
6. Maximum knee bend with maximum push.
7. Follow through and prepare to repeat.

Figure 57 *Double Poling with a Stride*

Running Bumps

Nearly all cross-country tracks which are prepared develop ups and downs, except those that cross lakes. The expert ski tourer and racer will make use of these bumps to propel himself forward. Simply maintaining pole rhythm, either diagonally or doubly, and making certain that the weighted ski is always on the downhill side of a bump is often sufficient to maintain good speed if the frequency of the bumps is relatively short. If the frequency is longer and the depressions deeper, a single stride and the use of double poling on the downhill side of a bump will often provide the inertia to rise over the next one. Maintaining this inertia is extremely important. Often under conditions where a skier has a lot of backslip in his wax, it is possible to utilize this inertia in a series of very short hopping steps, from one foot to the other, to clear the bump without having to resort to the herringbone or sidestepping maneuver.

For me, straight running over rolling terrain is far more enjoyable than running on a dead flat, such as a snow-covered lake, because of the extra assistance that the effort-conscious skier can obtain from the slightest downgrade.

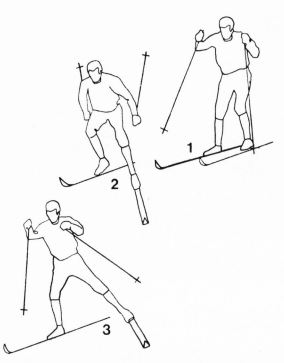

Figure 58 *Skating*
 1. Lift off one ski while poling.
 2. Push off hard on weighted ski.
 3. Transfer weight to raised ski and alternate.

Skating (see fig. 58)

It is far easier to skate on cross-country skis than on Alpine or downhill skis due to their light weight. Often on slight downgrades or on a flat with the wind behind you, with fast conditions, skating is an extremely efficient way of maintaining speed. The technique is obvious; the weight is transferred from ski to ski in a rhythmical way by pushing off from one ski to the other. Keeping relaxed and in constant motion is the mark of the real expert. Skating is excellent preparation for learning the step-around turn and can often be combined with the latter.

While a skater on skates can actually overlap one foot over the other, picking the rear foot from behind and placing it in front of the forward skate, the skier must place one ski alongside the other, and reach out with the inner ski, transfer his weight, and then repeat the motion. With practice, this can be done very gracefully and develop the same speed or inertia forward that comes from the speed skater's technique on ice in a corner. Practice skating on the flat and then converting the normal "V" pattern into the skating turn. You will discover that you are able to maintain your speed, and control your direction with considerable precision. Only practice of this sort on the flat will develop the balance and rhythm which is so necessary for step-around turns while running downhill and for conversion from straight running to the sidestep traverse when approaching an upgrade.

CLIMBING

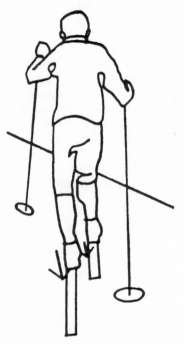

Figure 59 *Traversing*
Edge skis into the hill to prevent backslip.

Traversing

The easiest way to climb hills on cross-country skis is to eliminate the hill. This one can do by selecting a line which is relative to the fall line of the slope and is therefore less steep. Just as the whitewater canoe racer must judge whether it is faster to take the longer route around a corner where the water is moving faster on the outside or to paddle at a slower speed across the shorter distance on the inside of the corner, the cross-country ski tourer must judge whether more effort will be used in moving at a higher speed on a longer gradual traverse or in moving at a slow speed on a shorter but steeper traverse. This exercise in judgment can only be learned through experience, and certainly

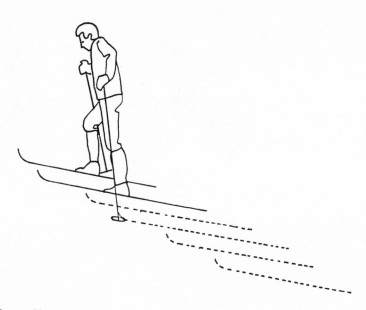

Figure 60
Sidestepping While Traversing or Modified Sidestep
Especially appropriate when loose snow
makes a direct sidestepping approach difficult

accounts for a great deal of the difference in effort required between the expert and the novice skier to cover the same distance. Generally, I like to maintain my forward momentum and will often select the longer route for this reason. Unlike the summertime hiker, the cross-country ski tourer can traverse slopes on the contour very easily since, by edging his skis, he makes a level track for himself. Of course, this is not true under very hard snow conditions. But, with that exception, it generally is. Very fast horizontal traverses on the contour can be made by a skating motion, keeping the uphill ski on the ground and periodically transferring the weight to the downhill ski and allowing it to travel away momentarily from the track towards the fall line and then lifting it back. This one-ski skate can move one incredibly fast directly across a slope and it is useful in the mountains for traversing steep snow fields where exposure time to avalanche hazards must be minimized.

Figure 61 *The Further Your Reach Around, the Less Apt You Are to Slip Back*

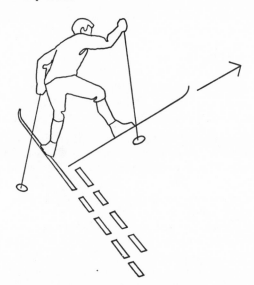

Figure 62 *Changing Direction While Traversing*
1. Lift uphill ski around.
2. Use edging and poles to prevent backslip.
3. Lift other ski around.

Generally, the diagonal stride can be used on the upgrade, gradually shortening the pace or length of stride as the gradient increases. When the traverse has been carried as far as it can go, the direction is reversed by a partial kick turn, as illustrated in figure 62. This is an easy maneuver and can be accomplished even on extremely steep slopes. Certainly, this form of traversing is the least tiring way to ascend any grade.

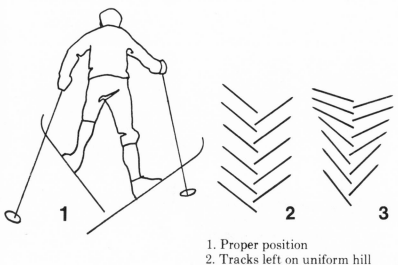

1. Proper position
2. Tracks left on uniform hill
3. Tracks left on hill which gets steeper

Figure 63 *The Herringbone for Hill Climbing*

The Herringbone (see fig. 63)

The herringbone maneuver is familiar to the Alpine skier and is basically self-explanatory. It is the most tiring of any way to climb, but often is the quickest means for ascending a short, steep slope. Personally, I avoid the herringbone whenever possible, preferring a modified sidestep instead to maintain a steep traverse line (see figure 60).

89

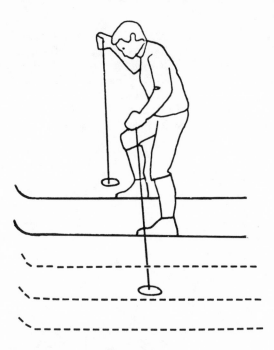

Figure 64 *Direct Uphill Sidestepping*
Edge the skis into the hill to prevent slipping
forward or backward.

Sidestepping (see fig. 64)

Sidestepping is a slow, but somewhat less tiring, procedure
than the herringbone for ascending steep slopes. Since there is
little tendency for the ski to slide in its track, the skier simply
transfers his weight from one ski to the other, reaching as high
with the uphill ski as he can on practically each step. Often in
deep powder snow, this can be a terribly fatiguing process
because, with each step, quantities of snow are loosened and fall
on the downhill ski. Edging to provide a ledge to support the
weight is made very difficult under these conditions. Because the
stability of the track is undermined in this way, I prefer to
advance either forward or backwards when sidestepping so that a

portion of the ski is always falling in unbroken snow. (See fig. 60: The Modified Sidestep.) This is possible in extremely deep snow conditions, and is very easy on hard snow. Here reliance is placed on one's wax to prevent backslip, but the weight is continually transferred to a ski which at least is partially resting in unbroken snow on an undisturbed platform.

While running on varying terrain, the sidestep modified to involve only a small deviation from the straight up path on the fall line is an extremely fast way to climb over steep grades. Making many small steps, crouching low, it is often possible to ascend virtually directly up the fall line with the skis angled as little as 25 degrees from the direction of travel. A hopping motion in which the skis "pitter-patter" over the snow, while remaining stationary for only an instant, is often extremely effective in maintaining one's forward inertia.

Obviously, waxing (see Chapter 6) is extremely important for hill climbing. The novice skier will discover this long before he discovers the importance of waxing for the diagonal stride on the level. Watching the experienced racer climbing hills is extremely revealing. His weight is carried on the balls of his feet, well forward over his skis in a slight crouch. The tempo of his stride is quickened as is his poling motion. The expert can climb hills with wax that the novice would find had excessive backslip. While touring, I find a variety of techniques useful for preventing backslip when climbing hills at slow speed. If the snow is firm old snow and one's wax is too hard for the conditions and thus has excessive backslip, a sharp slamming action while placing one foot in front of the other and care in transferring the weight to the forward ski gradually and uniformly will enable one to climb quite steep gradients without backslip. If the opposite condition exists, where the wax is too soft for soft snow, it will only succeed in loading up the bottom of the ski with snow and ice if one uses this method. Here it is advisable to place the ski gently on the snow, rolling forward on the balls of the feet so as to transfer one's weight extremely gradually, thus avoiding backslip. The ski should then be slid on the snow to prevent snow build-up. This kind of wax can be very frustrating because not only does it have the danger of icing and snow build-up but also, in contradiction, excessive backslip. Experienced, expert skiers can learn to overcome a less-than-perfect waxing job during hill climbing. Excessive backslip, even while running on the flat, can

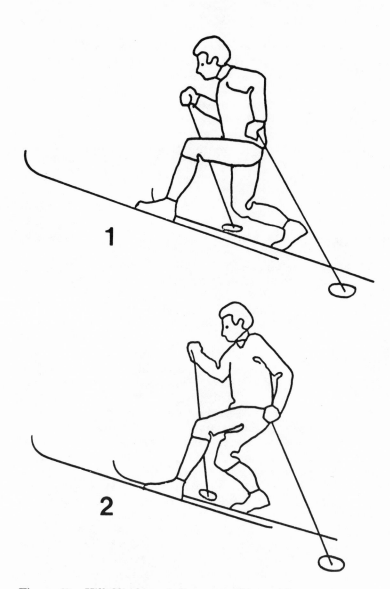

Figure 65 *Hill Climbing* 1. Proper position with
weight forward and poles behind.
2. Improper position. Weight too far back.

be overcome by extending less and therefore taking shorter strides. However, this is extremely tiring and a less than desirable experience.

The Change-Up

The change-up, or *passgang* is a maneuver used by competitors when hill climbing to gain momentary relaxation from the diagonal stride and is nothing more or less than the omission of a poling action while taking several short gliding steps before resuming normal diagonal poling. The only purpose of this maneuver is to allow the skier a momentary rest from the poling and running action of the diagonal stride. The skier should straighten his body, relaxing his back and shoulder muscles while breathing deeply. The legs should be carried in a slight crouch through the short strides to maintain forward inertia.

Maneuvers such as the change-up sound complicated, but are in fact extremely simple and every skier - even the novice tour skier - will soon include them and double poling in his normal diagonal technique without even thinking about it.

Figure 66   The Fundamental Maneuver for the Downhill Ski

Figure 67   *Straight Running in the Telemark Position*

DOWNHILL TECHNIQUE

As far as I am concerned, touring skis were primarily designed
for sliding downhill and so I seek out slopes covered in soft,
unbroken snow at every opportunity. Many novice cross-country
skiers have found this aspect of the sport the most frustrating
and difficult to deal with. This is because of the lack of stability
they feel with the lightweight equipment, compared with that
used for Alpine or downhill skiing and, in addition to that, their
ignorance about downhill technique. In this section, I will
describe maneuvers which should make it possible for the ski
tourer to not only overcome every slope, but obtain great
enjoyment in the process.

Figure 68 *The Conventional Downhill Crouch Offers Little Fore and Aft Stability*

Straight Running

Cross-country touring and racing bindings alike, being hinged at the ball of the foot, offer no fore and aft stability in themselves to the skier. Therefore, the skier must either move his feet apart in the fore and aft direction or simply balance with his feet together. The latter is entirely possible if the track or snow conditions are smooth and unvarying. The competition skier can assume the same crouch as the downhill Alpine skier, placing all his weight on the heels of his skis and thus gaining a measure of fore and aft stability. Normally, for straight running, a position

Figure 69   *Straight Running*
Note how the skier's weight is back on his skis.
The poles may be tucked over the skier's thighs to
reduce drag.

Figure 70   *Straight Running Over Bumps*
Keep your head as level as possible.

with one ski slightly ahead of the other ski is more desirable due
to the greatly increased resistance to falling which is gained by
having one's feet apart.

Lateral stability for the cross-country skier is obtained by a
reasonably wide stance in which up to a foot or more is allowed
between the skis. Lateral stability can also be obtained through
use of the arms and poles as balancing devices similar to a
tightwire walker's pole. The skilled skier will develop a narrow
track, one ski ahead of the other, and remain fully in control by
twisting his poles outward at the wrist to maintain his balance. It
is useful to practice these techniques on a gradual slope in both

broken and unbroken snow, and in a very short time one will discover how to maintain stability and to recover by either foot position or pole action from its momentary loss. I like to alternate the lead ski backwards and forwards at all times, constantly shifting weight from one ski to the other to optimize the glide obtained from slight variations in the snow surface. As we discuss the steered turns, you will understand more of the reasons for this.

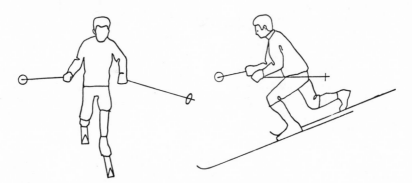

Figure 71   *Straight Running - Telemark Position*
The poles and arms are used for balance although, for straight running, a wider stance like this helps give stability.

Telemark Position Straight Running (see fig. 71)

For straight running over bumpy ground or where sliding conditions are unpredictable, as with windblown or drifted snow, the telemark position should always be used. One ski is moved far forward, forming a right angle with the knee of the forward leg. The knee of the trailing leg nearly touches the trailing ski so that the shin of this leg is parallel to the ski. Since this position is tiring to hold for a long time, one should get in the habit of constantly alternating legs. For straight running, the narrow stance needed for the telemark turn is not required. The telemark position, therefore, is useful even for the novice. As his balance improves, he will find that gradually he can narrow his stance or distance between the skis.

Figure 72 *Step-Around Turn*
The skier should be crouched lower.

TURNING AND THE TELEMARK
The Step-Turn (see fig. 72)

The first and most fundamental turn for the cross-country ski tourer to make, while running downhill, is the step-around turn or skating-turn, which was practiced on the flat. In this maneuver, the skier sits back slightly with his knees bent in a crouch and his weight on the heels of his skis, and picks one ski up a time, moving to the left or right. The key to learning this maneuver is to make short steps with regular, rhythmical frequency. Often, it is possible to speed up one's rate of progress by using the step-turn since, with each step, one is pushing off of the trailing ski. This is the major disadvantage of the step-turn for many novices because their desire to turn, in the first place, is quite often the result of a desire to slow down their rate of progress, not speed it up; therefore, while they may manage to accomplish the step-turn to avoid an obstacle, they must resort to sitting down to stop. For this reason, I recommend practicing the step-turn on very gradual slopes where one's speed can be controlled simply by the depth of the snow until the skier develops real confidence in avoiding obstacles at reasonably high speeds. When executed by an expert, the step-turn can be quite graceful if the poling action is coordinated with it or when the skier is carrying his poles with his arms tucked in front of his body, his knees well bent, and the rhythm of each step kept uniform. Combining the step-turn with a skating maneuver on a slight downgrade is excellent practice. The ski should be lifted quickly, high above the snow, so that it does not catch or drag on the loose snow in between each step. Developing split second reflexes in maneuvering one's skis in this way only comes with experience and the novice is bound to occasionally misjudge and get a ski tip caught under a low branch or on the wrong side of a small sapling. Practice the maneuver in increasingly difficult circumstances and accept the fact that eventually you will misjudge and break a ski tip. Of course, the chances of doing this are measurably increased when using lightweight racing skis which have virtually no resistance when they encounter an immovable object, such as a tree.

Steered Turns by Edging (see fig. 73 & 74)

Due to their very flexible tips, cross-country skis when edged by rotating the ankles will, in deep snow, quickly knife into the snow in the direction of rotation, moving the skier swiftly in that direction. To practice edged turns, try straight running in two or three inches of soft snow, one foot slightly ahead of the other, and rotate the ankles left and right, allowing one turn to start and then interrupting it before it is completed. The skis should be held close together during this maneuver to minimize the danger of "spread-eagling" on the snow. For this reason, edging should not be attempted until the skier has developed reasonable confidence in balancing with his feet close together and has mastered the use of the poles as balancing devices. In using the poles, do not raise the hands high above the head; keep them no higher than shoulder height and twist the poles outward by wrist action. You will soon discover that this edge turning technique is

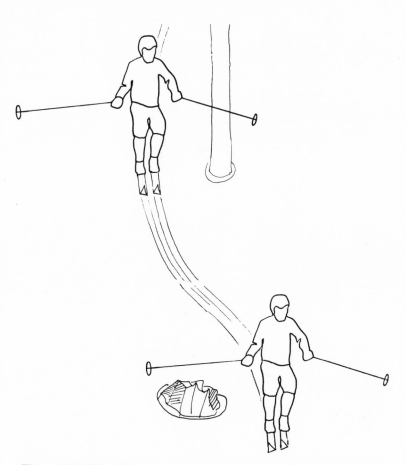

Figure 73   *Edge Turns*

an effective means of braking when descending steep slopes in deep powder snow. Often in descending a trail where the track is broken out, I will leave the trail and enter the unbroken snow on the side to avoid buiding up excessive speed. If the edging is exaggerated, the instep of the boot acts as a drag in the snow and will provide most effective braking. In edging the skis, always turn them in the direction of the fall line, not away from it. Turning away from it will bring the skier to a very abrupt stop quite often throwing him into a sideways downhill fall. With

Figure 74 *Edge Turn to the Left*

practice, one can slide from bump to bump running towards the
fall line in deep snow, at substantial speed, avoiding obstacles
with great precision. The lead ski should be on the fall line side,
or direction of turn, in every case and the trailing ski simply falls
into the groove cut by the tip of the lead ski. More advanced
turns, such as the telemark, are simply elaborations on this very
simple edging technique, although they offer far greater steering
control. In practicing this kind of maneuver, constantly change
directions so that it becomes natural to respond with the
downhill ski when wishing to change direction.

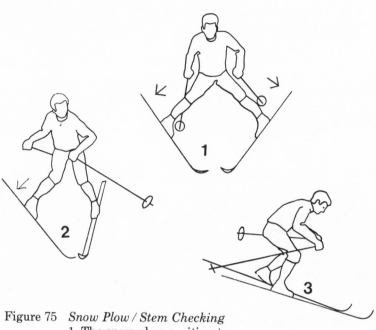

Figure 75 *Snow Plow / Stem Checking*
    1. The snow plow position to
    2. The weight shift for a stem turn to
    3. The traverse

Snow Plows and Stemming (see fig. 75)

Conventional snow plows, stem turns, and even parallel Christianias, such as are used in Alpine skiing, are often used on cross-country skis to control speed on packed snow conditions. I believe that these techniques, which involve sliding the ski perpendicular to its longitudinal axis, are hard on the equipment, particularly the bindings and ski bottoms, and their use should be minimized. Nevertheless, they are often the easiest way to check one's speed on certain snow conditions. The skier's weight should be back on his heels, his knees well cocked forward in the snow plow. Unlike Alpine skiing, the use of these techniques with Nordic equipment is really for experts who have already mastered the problems of balance with narrow and lightweight equipment.

Figure 76 *The Ski Glissade*
Grasp the poles low, close to their baskets.
Crouch low.
Combine this maneuver with a partial snow
plow under hard snow - narrow trail conditions
when you need to check your speed.

The Ski Glissade (see fig. 76)

This speed-checking maneuver is often combined with a
partial snow plow and is an excellent means of descending a
narrow trail with hard snow conditions. If you ever find yourself
stuck in a snowmobile track, try this. The whole trick is to get
very low and grasp the poles very close to their baskets, both in
one hand. Naturally, metal poles substantially reduce the risk of
breakage. This technique is exactly the same as a
mountaineer's glissade on his boots with an ice axe and requires
that a substantial portion of his weight be transferred to the
poles if the braking action is to be effective.

Double Pole Jump Turn (see fig. 77)

The jump turn is a very convenient means of changing
direction and checking one's speed in extremely difficult snow
conditions where it is impossible to steer the skis. Heavy wet
snow or breakable crust conditions virtually rule out all other
means of controlling downhill speed. In the double pole jump
turn, the skier starts out in a relatively flat traverse of the slope
or, in other words, nearly perpendicular to the fall line. When his
speed has reached no more than five miles per hour, he brings
both poles forward together, planting them with the baskets
touching, a few inches from the tips of both skis on the downhill
side. He then springs forward, pivoting on his poles and turning,
while airborne, to a position perpendicular to the fall line with
the skis pointed in the reverse direction, some distance down the

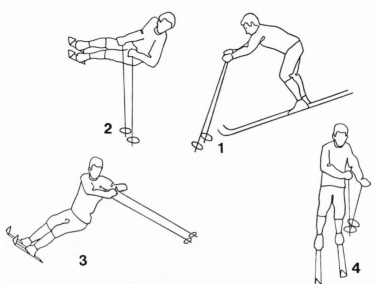

Figure 77 *The Double Pole Jump Turn*
  1. Crouch and plant both poles approximately one foot downhill and directly opposite your tips.
  2. Jump up, arresting your motion with your poles and pivoting around them in the downhill direction.
  3. Push off while airborne and with your skis perpendicular to the fall line.
  4. Land perpendicular to the fall line, absorbing the shock by crouching. Edge the skis into the hill to prevent sliding.

slope. On very steep slopes, it is possible to drop twenty feet or more vertically in this maneuver. Cross-country and touring equipment is extremely suitable, due to its light weight, and little strain is placed on the skis or bindings throughout the entire maneuver. Important points to remember are timing the leap to follow the placement of the poles all in one motion and to quickly rotate the body into a virtually horizontal position relative to the slope, pushing off with the poles to increase distance downhill and dropping down into the snow in a vertical position, poised and ready to prevent further sliding of the skis by edging them into the hill. At first, you will find that your feet

Figure 78 *The Ultimate Single Pole Jump Turn*
Sig Buchmayr on the Headwall,
Tuckerman's Ravine, Mount Washington, N.H.

slide out from under you, causing you to land on your side, or alternatively you will fall over after landing due to too much downhill inertia of the upper body. The maneuver is easier to do on a steep slope than on a relatively flat slope. Practicing off the edge of small bump which has a steep incline beyond it is perhaps the easiest way to begin. The steeper the slope, the more time the skier has while in flight to position his body for the landing. Upon landing, the knees should be flexed and arms brought low to generally lower the center of gravity. With practice, the skier will be able to link jump turns, never coming to a complete rest between them. It is possible to negotiate very steep and narrow trails in this way. While doing jump turns in deep powder snow is great fun, it is far more difficult to plant the poles positively under these conditions, especially the ones with small baskets that are so common today.

Single Pole Jump Turn (see fig. 78)

The principles of the single pole jump turn are identical to that of the double pole version, except that only the downhill pole is planted. Sometimes the uphill pole is planted to assist in getting the skier airborne and then withdrawn immediately as the pivot on the downhill pole is commenced. I believe it to be significantly more difficult than the double pole version and would recommend mastering the latter first.

Figure 79   *Turning Towards the Fall Line in the Telemark*

Telemark Turn (see figs. 79 & 80)

The telemark is the basic downhill steered turn which can be accomplished on cross-country touring skis under nearly all conditions, except where the surface is hard. In the telemark, the skier relies on his poles for lateral stability, bringing his skis

Figure 80 *Good Telemark Position*

together in a narrow stance, advancing one ski far forward so that the knee of the trailing leg virtually touches the trailing ski. This is the telemark position which is used by ski jumpers to control their fore and aft balance from the moment of impact until they have crossed the transition from the jumping hill to the flat. At this phase of the ski jump, there is a considerable tendency for the jumper to either go on his face or sit on his behind and the telemark position provides ultimate stability against this happening. I use the telemark position for straight downhill running (see fig. 61) when the terrain is extremely bumpy and rough just because of this ability to provide effective fore and aft stability. In this position, it is possible to run your lead ski right into a pile of brush without falling on your face in the process.

The telemark is more than one turn; it is a whole technique for controlling one's descent on skis and bindings in which the heel may be raised. Its basic body and ski positions are appropriate for:

1. straight running
2. stop turns on the flat
3. uphill or stop turns from a traverse
4. uphill, stop turns from a direct descent, and

5.   downhill turns for directional control from a traverse.

Generally it is best to learn to telemark in the order listed above. Find a gentle slope (around 5 degrees) with a flat out-run, preferably when conditions are such that there are 4 to 6 inches of light powder on top of a smooth (no ruts) and firm base. The less soft snow there is, the more gentle the slope may be. I have seen complete novices learn the telemark on 1 or 2 inches of snow on a virtually flat pitch.

Begin by straight running in the telemark position (see figs. 67 & 71) alternating the forward leg with the rear leg in an easy rhythm until you are perfectly confident of being able to maintain your balance. As you sink into the telemark position, keep your weight evenly distributed between your skis. With more experience, and when turning, you will discover that equal weight distribution is not always desirable, but at this stage and in straight running, I find it helps in achieving the proper telemark position with one's body erect. As your balance improves, gradually narrow your stance until your skis are close together. Resist the natural temptation to raise your arms over your head; keep them well below your shoulders and reach out with your poles. Your poles are to you exactly what the tight rope walker's pole is to him. An excellent exercise is to omit your poles altogether until you can alternate telemark positions smoothly in a narrow stance while maintaining your balance by your arms only and controlling precisely the weight distribution between your skis.

Stop Telemark

First, try this turn on the level after a short descent sufficient to build up a small amount of speed (5 mph). From the telemark position, exert a small amount of twisting effort on the forward ski to induce a turn in the direction of the rear ski (i.e. left ski forward to turn right and vice versa). If it does not turn immediately, try shifting your weight slightly to the rear and edging the ski. Continue the turn in one direction, coming to a stop. Just as a cyclist must bank in a corner, you must lean slightly toward the center of the turn to avoid being carried over your skis onto your face.

After mastering this turn in both directions, try it on a gradual slope coming to a stop from a gradual traverse. Turn away from the fall line so that your speed is constantly diminishing through-out the maneuver. In other words, if you are crossing the slope from left to right, advance your *left* ski and turn it *uphill*. You may find it so effective a stopping technique that you end up pointing uphill and begin to slip backwards. Don't despair, as you will soon learn how to control this effect.

Gradually increase your descent line until it is parallel to the fall line when you begin the stop telemark. When you have become quite confident in being able to initiate the stop telemark from any direction and with varying amounts of speed, try doing it without poles and even with your hands clasped behind your back!

Downhill Telemark Swings (see fig. 81)

Unlike the stop telemark, downhill telemarks increase the skier's speed as he continually turns toward the fall line. Unlike all downhill or Alpine technique, the telemark permits changes in direction without checking speed. This accounts for the very rewarding skiing to be obtained on even gentle slopes through use of this technique.

To begin the downhill telemark, advance the uphill ski while in a gentle traverse and swing it toward the fall line. Again, you must lean toward the center of the turn, like a cyclist, but this time you must also stay forward, trying to maintain at least one half of your weight on the forward ski. You will be surprised how your speed picks up quickly even on the most gentle slope. Alternate your position immediately after completing the turn in pre-paration for the next one in the opposite direction. Control your speed by extending each turn partially into a stop telemark as far as is necessary.

To develop confidence in swinging toward the fall line, I re-commend that you alternate swings while virtually straight run-ning on a *very* gentle slop. Initiate each swing and then alternate your position almost before it has begun so that you leave a con-tinuous "S" track. Also, try this without poles and with your hands behind your back. One advantage is that you may maintain a reasonably wide stance whereas, in a more complete turn, your skis naturally come together and offer very little lateral stability.

Weight distribution between the forward and aft ski is variable.

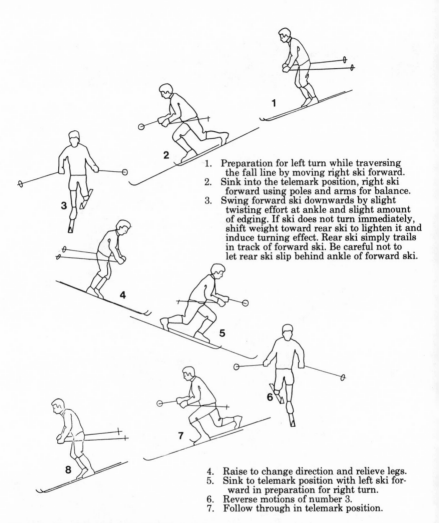

1. Preparation for left turn while traversing the fall line by moving right ski forward.
2. Sink into the telemark position, right ski forward using poles and arms for balance.
3. Swing forward ski downwards by slight twisting effort at ankle and slight amount of edging. If ski does not turn immediately, shift weight toward rear ski to lighten it and induce turning effect. Rear ski simply trails in track of forward ski. Be careful not to let rear ski slip behind ankle of forward ski.

4. Raise to change direction and relieve legs.
5. Sink to telemark position with left ski forward in preparation for right turn.
6. Reverse motions of number 3.
7. Follow through in telemark position.

Figure 81   *The Downhill Telemark*

Ideally, it is equal as in straight running; however, I have found that in very deep snow and when moving a high speed it is sometimes necessary to shift one's weight more to the rear ski and allow the forward ski to simply plane and carve a path for the trailing ski. At other times when moving more slowly and on firmer surfaces, it can be quite the other way around, with the

Figure 82 *Turning Away From the Fall Line in the Telemark*

trailing ski simply following the fully weighted forward ski. One can only experiment with this and reach one's own conclusions. Of course, in each position transfer of the telemark, the rear ski must be substantially unweighted to be brought forward, but the duration of this unweighting may only be a few seconds as the transfer is initiated.

Figure 83 *The Less Snow the More One Tends to Weight the Forward Ski*

As your confidence grows, you will discover that the telemark enables you to control the direction and rate of your descent with infinite precision. Few thrills, to me, compare with linked downhill telemarks in deep powder as the snow pummels your chest and you are constantly reaching for a new "line" to maintain and control your speed.

Figure 84 *The Most Common Telemark Fault: Arms Raised Over Shoulders*

Learning to telemark in dense woods where stable snow exists for a large percentage of the time is very useful. In the northeast, soft powder conditions often remain in hardwood forests long after the snow has become old and hard or windblown on the open slopes. Because the telemark offers so much accuracy to the skier, it is possible to ski at very high speeds through trees spaced

Figure 85   *Another Common Telemark Fault: The Rigid Forward Knee*

only a few feet apart. Slopes to avoid are those where there is underbrush. The typical Vermont "sugar bush", or stand of pure maples, is ideal as the ground is usually clear of shrubbery. The reader should be forewarned that this kind of skiing *does* involve risks since moving at high speeds near immovable objects always is hazardous.

Figure 86   *Goggles Sometimes Make It Easier to Keep One's Eyes Open when Straight Running in the Brush*

Common Mistakes in the Telemark

1. Advancing the rear foot too soon or when too heavily weighted, which tends to make the skier "bolt" downhill or sit back and ultimately sit down.
2. Leaning inward excessively. When learning at slow speeds, this is a common problem, somewhat alleviated by facing out toward the fall line with the upper body.
3. Raising the arms over one's head, thus losing their stabilizing influence. Eventually one must develop good balance while keeping arms *and* poles close to the body if one is to learn to telemark in dense woods. (see fig. 84.)
4. Straightening the forward knee and becoming stiff which makes subtle variations in fore and aft weighting of the skis difficult or impossible. (see fig. 85.)

The Double Telemark

Paired telemarks on broad open slopes are great fun (see fig. 29). Each skier carries both poles in his or her outer arm and, interlocking arms, coordinates telemark turns with his or her partner. A double set of perfectly matched tracks down a long powder slope is an amazing sight indeed!

General

It is always advisable to remove the pole wrist straps from your hands so that if a basket gets caught on a branch, you do not end up with a dislocated shoulder. Practice first in open country and gradually move into orchards, where the trees are well spaced or in areas where only small flexible saplings exist. Know your capabilities so that you can judge instantly your ability to complete a turn in time to avoid an obstacle. Only by practice do you develop this knowledge. If you make a mistake, use your arms to cushion the impact and to protect your head. Normally, I find it possible to do a side-fall uphill while telemarking if an emergency situation arises. However, often in reaching with the forward ski, it is necessary to lean the body downhill in order to precipitate the turn and during these moments one is very

117

exposed. If the slope is so steep that a fall could propel you head first towards a tree at this point, I would advise abandoning the turn and continuing the traverse. I have found that ideal telemark conditions in steep wooded slopes do *not* present a tremendous obstacle, even to the novice skier, who can make long flat downhill traverses, edge to a stop, do a kick turn, and reverse his direction through even dense woods, with his speed always under complete control. For this reason, even in a party of greatly varying abilities, seeking out the ideal telemark hill is great fun for all.

For all cross-country downhill turns, the skier should anticipate the turn by making turning movements sooner than he believes will be necessary, just as the Alpine skier must make his turn well before approaching the slalom gate so that his delayed change in direction coincides exactly with the gate pole. This is fundamental procedure in many sports, such as auto racing and hydroplane racing, where the turn is initiated prematurely - or what seems like prematurely - so that the change in direction occurs at the precise instant the obstacle is passed. Experimentation on an open slope doing telemarks between bamboo poles is the only way to gain a full appreciation of this fact.

FALLING (see fig. 87)

Falling on cross-country skis is inevitable for skiers of all abilities. Generally, one falls in one of three ways: either sitting down between one's skis; falling to one side; or pitching forward on one's face. Surprisingly, the last alternative is often the least injurious to the skier and his equipment. Sitting down sometimes results in a broken ski if one sits directly on the tail of the ski very suddenly, but otherwise is quite an acceptable method of bringing oneself to an abrupt stop at slow speeds, or even high speeds. However, if traveling at very high speed, the skier should attempt, as he sits down, to slide both skis perpendicular to the fall line and keep them together, offering a plowing and thus braking effect and protecting the skier from bushes, trees, or other obstacles which may be before him.

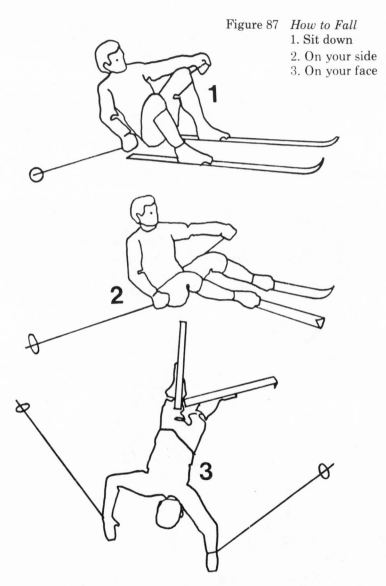

Figure 87 *How to Fall*
1. Sit down
2. On your side
3. On your face

Surprisingly, No. 3 is often the best way.

Falling on one's side often results in a broken pole or a wrenched shoulder and is, for me, the least desirable way of falling, but often inevitable when practicing maneuvers which require a great degree of balance, such as the telemark.

When pitching forwards on one's face, the thing to remember is to land on one's forearms if possible and allow one's skis to spread so that the tips end up pointing backwards. Needless to say, this maneuver is to be avoided, if at all possible, in breakable crust conditions, where one can receive severe cuts on one's face. Generally, it is most successfully accomplished in deep powder snow and merely

1. Incorrect - Skis are not perpendicular to the fall line.
Weight is not over skis.

2. Correct - Note how the weight of the skier is over the skis.

3. Best of All - The skier is able to stand up without removing pole wrist straps.

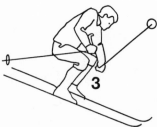

Figure 88 *How to Get Up*

120

results in the skier getting wet. Because of the freedom of movement provided by cross-country bindings, the mass of the skier's weight is allowed to carry forward beyond his skis, which usually spares the skis the full force of the impact and they are therefore not broken. It is when the moving mass of the skier is absorbed by the limber and flexible toes of the skis that they usually break. This can happen with very light racing skis when the racer leaves a broken track at very high speed and enters deep powder snow. The abrupt upturned tip on modern skis makes for a strong plowing action in deep snow. The older touring skis were more appropriate in this respect as they tended to slice through the snow more readily.

Regardless of what position the skier ends up in, he should roll onto his back and place his skis on the downhill side of his body, perpendicular to the fall line and preferably together. He should then move the center of gravity of his body over the skis to rise to his feet, using his poles for stability. He should avoid trying to raise himself entirely through pole effort; it often results in a broken pole and always results in more fatigue. If the skier is careful to move his center of gravity over the skis, it is often quite unnecessary to remove the wrist straps from the poles to regain his position on his feet.

An efficient way of regaining one's feet in extremely deep powder, especially on relatively flat terrain where it is more difficult to get one's weight over the skis, is to grasp both poles at the center to form an "x" and push up from this point.

Figure 89   *Always Avoid Getting Your Skis Wet as Usually They Will Ice Up Immediately*

OVERCOMING OBSTACLES

The cross-country ski tourer who seeks out unbroken snow is invariably confronted with obstacles of all sorts. In this section, I will attempt to describe maneuvers for overcoming these obstacles.

Stone Walls

If a wall is adequately covered with snow, approach the wall so that one's skis are as close to it as possible, and parallel to it, and raise the nearest ski as high as possible and place it directly on top of the wall and stand up on it, transferring the load to one's poles and to the upper leg until standing directly on top of the wall. Descending the other side can be done in the same fashion, or if the vertical height is too great, lean down and insert your pole into the snow on the opposite side of the wall and jump, with both feet parallel, into the snow. Great care must be taken in all such operations to be certain that neither ski lands partially on the wall or in a depression where it could break. Unless the wall is virtually buried in snow, do not attempt to run straight over it, as the stiffer tail of the skis will often break off about a foot from the end.

Wire Fences (see. fig. 90)

Wire fences which are low enough can be stepped over in the same way as a stone wall, but watch out for barbed wire. Grasping the wire with both hands, having placed both poles on the opposite side of the fence, provides some security against getting impaled as one lifts each leg over the fence. I often cross fences such as these by doing a kick-turn alongside the fence,

Figure 90   *Crossing Fence with a Kick Turn*
         A simple procedure for relatively low fences

and while rotating the ski, I pick it up and place it on the opposite side of the fence. Such techniques are only useful if the fence is quite low. Sagging wire fences can often be crossed by placing the ski across on the wire with the boot directly over the wire so that your entire weight can be transferred to the wire while balancing on your poles. Great care must be taken in getting off the fence from this position by holding one ski forward, slipping its tail beneath the wire and transferring the weight entirely to that ski so that no chance of snapping the tail of the other ski is taken.

Fence Jumping (see fig. 91)

Higher wire and wooden fences can be jumped from a standing position very easily, and I highly recommend practicing this technique for crossing all obstacles which do not have great thickness and which do not exceed shoulder height. Even the novice can quickly learn to jump obstacles up to elbow height and it is very useful knowledge to have as it enables one to avoid removing one's skis in deep snow or having to ski around much greater distances. Another advantage of this technique is that no damage is done to the fence as the skier's weight is only transmitted to the fence post itself.

The procedure is as follows. Stand with skis parallel to the fence and as close to it as seems comfortable; for me, this is approximately one foot from the edge of the closest ski. Remove both wrist straps from your hands and, placing the poles together, insert them very close to the outside ski, directly beside the boot. Then, place the free hand on top of the fence post and the opposite hand on top of the two poles. Leaning forward slightly, jump straight up, tucking the skis up as far as is possible, while rotating the weight of your whole body onto the hand resting on the fence post. Swing the skis together over the fence and land in the snow on the opposite side of the fence pointing in the reverse direction. The poles can normally be drawn along through this maneuver unless the fence is especially high, in which case it may be necessary to let go of them. If at first this seems like an insurmountable maneuver, practice jumping vertically along the fence without rotating the body until your confidence is at the stage where you can complete the

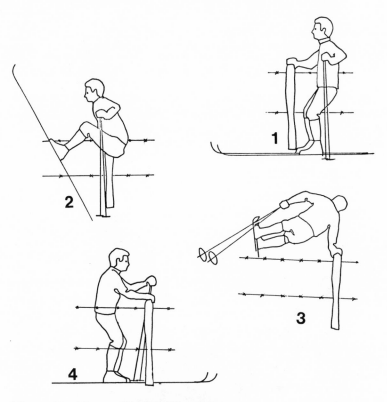

Figure 91   *How to Jump a Wire Fence*
1. Move parallel to the fence.
2. Jump straight up using poles and fence post to carry your weight.
3. Swing over the wire by pushing off your poles and pivoting over fence post.
4. Land on the opposite side cushioning the impact by use of one arm on the fence post

maneuver. I often find that I get half-way, skis perpendicular to the fence, and I am unable to complete the rotation because I have not either sufficient height or forward momentum. All is not lost at this stage, however, since with a little practice and holding onto your poles, which are still in the ground, you can balance on top of even a wire fence in this position by keeping in a crouch position with the skis tucked close to the body. Once in this position, holding onto the fence post with one hand, remove the two poles together with the other hand and place them in the snow on the opposite side of the fence. Then, carefully supporting the weight of your body and skis on both arms, rotate yourself to the ground. Just a little practice at this maneuver and you will find it far simpler than it sounds or looks. It is so much fun that I now go out of my way to find fences to jump.

Figure 92 *The Author "Going Out of His Way"*

Bare Stone Walls (see fig. 93)

Stone walls or other broad obstacles with no snow on them can be crossed without removing the skis by moving parallel to the wall and turning your back to it and, removing your poles, hop up onto it so as to place your seat on top of the wall, dangling

1. Approach the wall closely.

2. Sit down on top - if high, use your poles in one hand to boost your seat on to the top of it.

3. Lie back on the wall.

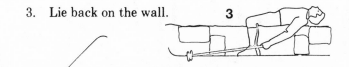

4. Raise your skis over your head and roll off

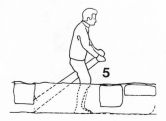

5. To the ground on the opposite side. Use your poles to lower yourself if the height is excessive.

Figure 93   *How to Cross a Stone Wall*

your skis below and parallel. From this position, roll back on your back, raise the skis over your head and turn over with a rolling motion, rotating your skis to fall back onto the snow on the opposite side of the wall and facing in the reverse direction. This is also an extremely easy maneuver to carry out and is often preferable to the removal of skis. I maintain that a good cross-country ski tourer should be free enough on his skis so that he can literally climb a tree with them on!

Crossing Roads

When it is necessary to cross a bare highway or gravel road, careful high steps - being certain not to slide the ski - should be used. Pick the ski neatly off the ground and place it softly down so that small pebbles of sand do not bruise the surface. Obviously, this is not easy on the wax and should be avoided whenever possible. Often, even in competition, however, the track does cross highways and one must be prepared for it.

Figure 94   *"Rolling Over" a Fence*

Crossing Branches and Shrubbery

As long as forward inertia is maintained, it is often possible to cross directly over piles of brush and shrubbery, but there is no easier way to break skis than attempting this with too little speed. Pick up the skis alternately, transferring the weight from one to the other, and avoid getting your tips caught or entangled in the branches. As long as your speed is maintained, there is relatively little chance of breaking skis this way.

Figure 95 *Waxing Kit* Note scraper, waxing cork, adjustable spare tip, and belt pack.

6   WAXING

Unlike Alpine skiing, where modern skis have virtually relegated waxing to the competition section entirely, waxing for all cross-country skiers is important. Trying a pair of perfectly waxed skis and seeing how it is possible to move straight up a 20 degrees slope without resorting to the herringbone, and then shoot down the other side with great speed is quite unbelievable to the novice. Learning to wax perfectly for all snow conditions is extremely difficult. In fact, no one has yet done it! Everyone makes mistakes in waxing, especially when conditions are changeable, as they often are.

The principle of cross-country waxing is that when the ski is placed on the snow and weighted, as the skier pushes off during his stride or when climbing a hill, microscopic fragments of the crystalline structured snow (or ice) press into the wax, which is soft, and produce friction. When the ski is then slid forward, the friction between the snow and the ski generates enough heat to melt these fragments, leaving a smooth surface which slips easily. It sounds unbelievable, but it works.

Generally it is easier to wax for cold new snow conditions than for warm wet or icy old snow conditions. This is true for the novice tourer who is interested in preventing backslip, but may be untrue for the expert racer who is primarily interested in good slide for speed.

Waxes vary in hardness, with the very hardest being used for soft new snow at very cold temperatures and the very softest, which are called *klisters,* being used on old crusted or wet snow at higher temperatures. These waxes are called surface waxes and are generally applied over a *base* and *base wax* which helps them adhere.

Except for competition, where track conditions can vary dramatically and sliding speed is essential, most tour skiers enjoying an afternoon tour or some bushwhacking are only interested in maintaining reasonable slide and avoiding excessive backslip. Since wet slushy and hard frozen icy conditions are generally to be avoided on this kind of outing, most tour skiers will find that they only need two or three kinds of harder waxes for skiing in unbroken snow. Most small wax kits sold by many manufacturers have a fully adequate range for the beginning skier. As you become more proficient and experiment more, you will accumulate a vast collection of esoteric waxes in a great chest which hopefully will never leave the back of your car. Ninety percent of my chest I never use because complete knowledge about the characteristics of a few waxes is really more useful. Waxing is a subtle art and the thickness and smoothness of the applied wax can have equal or more importance than its hardness or other chemical properties. The mystique associated with waxing for competition is immense. During my school day races, many team coaches waxed the competitors skis for them and would not allow them to know what was used! Many tricks to fool the opposition were devised, such as putting hard wax in containers color coded for soft wax to induce them to use it!

Every skier should learn to wax for himself or herself as nothing is more tiresome than waxing many pairs of skis belonging to others and then getting blamed if they stick or ice up. Everyone moves differently on skis which makes wax work differently for different people.

The Base

New skis usually come with a bare hardwood bottom or a very light brown tinted surface sealer which is intended to minimize changes in the moisture content of the wood during shipment and storage. This must be removed with light sandpaper or fine steel wool (or by sliding for a day on crusty snow) before waxes are applied. Increasingly, ski shops are applying a *base* to the skis they sell as an extra service, but I recommend that every skier learn how to do it as he or she will have to replace it many times throughout the normal life of the skis. It is a simple task which is done only to protect the wood of the ski from water and abrasion from icy snow. For the tour skier who skis exclusively on soft snow, the base may last an entire season or longer, while one day under crusty conditions can ruin any base. In fact, sharp icy crust can ruin the touring skis themselves rather quickly.

The base material most commonly used is a pine tar or derivative of same, commonly called *grundvalla.* One buys this in small cans (approximately $2.00 each) at any ski shop. Some brands will suggest that no heating or burning is required, but I recommend that all base material be "cooked" into the ski bottom by heating it with a torch until it bubbles or boils on top of the wood. In this way, it is forced into the fibers. The procedure is as follows: obtain a propane hand torch or other form of blow torch, preferably with a wide spreading tip although this is not absolutely necessary. Placing the warm skis (never apply a torch to cold skis), cleaned to bare wood, upside down in a horizontal position; spread the pine tar or grundvalla on quite thickly, using an old rag, not worrying about the dribbles that run under the ski to the top surface as these can be easily cleaned off with a rag moistened in turpentine after you have finished. It is best not to do this operation over fine rugs or floors, etc. Next, light the torch and, holding it several inches away, gently warm the entire length of both skis, gradually raising the temperature of the base until it is quite hot to touch. Then train the torch on a small area at one end and get the base material to boil in place. Just before it flames or just after, wipe this spot with an old towel with a single wipe, and remove the excess material. Work in this way from one end of each ski to the other end, doing only a small portion at a time. I find I can do only about four inches of a racing ski, and about four inches by one half the width of a touring ski with each wipe. If you try to do more, the base material will cool too quickly and not wipe off. Keep the torch in your left hand and the old towel in your right. You may find it easier to lean the skis against a bench and their tails against a

Figure 96 *Waxing Up Under the Foot*
One means of reducing backslip

wood cleat nailed to the floor or a wall so that they do not move with your wiping strokes. It may seem that you take off more than you leave on, but what is left on is what is important. One small can of pine tar or grundvalla usually will do three or four pairs of skis. My father used to paint the grundvalla on and leave the skis in hot sun where it could bake in slowly over several days. The finished base should feel smooth and dry and not excessively sticky. Never "burn in" a base on skis that have plastic edges. Some of the new skis with synthetic bottoms do permit use of a torch, but great care must be exercised to prevent damaging them.

Base Waxing

Waxes can be applied directly to the base or a very thin layer of base wax or binder (also called ground wax or *grundvox)* can be applied first. Base wax waterproofs the base and improves the bond of surface waxes. You buy it in small tubes and put very little on, rubbing it lightly on the surface and then smoothing it out with the heel of your hand or a cork. When finished, it should be so thin an application that you are only able to see your fingerprint in it. I find many base waxes to be rubbery and difficult to smooth and very often don't bother with them for this reason. However, there is no question that they do make surface waxes hold better and do make your base last longer. Since removing wax from the ski removes the base wax as well, it is necessary to replace it each time you rewax.

Surface Waxing

Surface waxes or running waxes are applied directly out of their tubes by rubbing them back and forth across the ski or up and down. Softer waxes or klisters are spread on like paste, using a stick of wood to smooth them. I do not recommend melting any cross-country waxes as one often does with Alpine or downhill paraffin because this can change their hardness characteristics. Rub the tube very lightly, putting a little on at a time and smooth it by using a cork or the heel of your hand (eventually you will build up callouses here). Use of a smoothing iron is popular with some people, but I never feel it is necessary. It tempts me to apply the wax too heavily, knowing that I will always be able to smooth it out with the iron.

Incidentally, I usually never carry a torch with me skiing, and have therefore recommended a propane version which always works, even at low temperatures, but is rather heavy. If you plan a several-day ski tour camping out, then the butane type, which is much lighter, is preferable. Take the precaution of prewarming the cylinder, however, if it is very cold.

Surface waxes are color coded by each manufacturer to indicate their relative hardness. Waxes are not manufactured for identical snow conditions by all manufacturers. It is, therefore, difficult to draw a comprehensive chart for all waxes, although this is done and may be of some value. I advise the novice cross-country skier to stick with one brand at first and learn how to use it.

Following is a waxing chart which I have reproduced that I believe to be the simplest one in existence. One does not even need to know the air temperature to use it and the complete novice

SCIA WAXING GUIDE

The proper wax for touring and cross-country skiing depends on the type of snow, how long it has settled on the ground and the moisture content. By selecting a number from each of the questions below, in sequence, you can identify a snow type. Waxes for that snow type are then listed in the table by manufacturer; only numbers corresponding to real snow types appear.

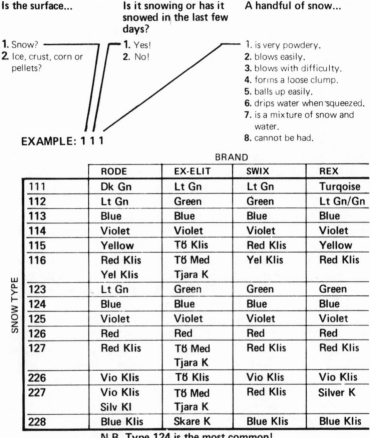

Is the surface...

1. Snow?
2. Ice, crust, corn or pellets?

Is it snowing or has it snowed in the last few days?

1. Yes!
2. No!

A handful of snow...

1. is very powdery.
2. blows easily.
3. blows with difficulty.
4. forms a loose clump.
5. balls up easily.
6. drips water when squeezed.
7. is a mixture of snow and water.
8. cannot be had.

EXAMPLE: 1 1 1

	BRAND			
SNOW TYPE	RODE	EX-ELIT	SWIX	REX
111	Dk Gn	Lt Gn	Lt Gn	Turqoise
112	Lt Gn	Green	Green	Lt Gn/Gn
113	Blue	Blue	Blue	Blue
114	Violet	Violet	Violet	Violet
115	Yellow	Tö Klis	Red Klis	Yellow
116	Red Klis Yel Klis	Tö Med Tjara K	Yel Klis	Red Klis
123	Lt Gn	Green	Green	Green
124	Blue	Blue	Blue	Blue
125	Violet	Violet	Violet	Violet
126	Red	Red	Red	Red
127	Red Klis	Tö Med Tjara K	Red Klis	Red Klis
226	Vio Klis	Tö Klis	Vio Klis	Vio Klis
227	Vio Klis Silv Kl	Tö Med Tjara K	Red Klis	Silver K
228	Blue Klis	Skare K	Blue Klis	Blue Klis

N.B. Type 124 is the most common!

Figure 97 *SCIA Waxing Guide*

should be able to answer the three questions it poses in selecting a wax. The four most popular waxes sold in North America are included. I suggest that the reader xerox this and tape it inside his waxing kit.

It should be recognized that combinations of several waxes may be appropriate. Often, softer klisters are used directly on the base and then covered with a thin layer of hard wax. This combination is one we used to favor when warming conditions were anticipated during a race. The more I have raced, however, the more concern I have developed for having good slide even at the expense of a little backslip and this combination often resulted in poor slide. Another trick is to rub a different wax under your feet for bite, and wax the rest of the ski primarily for slide.

To Remove Wax

I generally use a torch to remove wax because it is so fast. A hand scraper is also quite effective and is less apt to remove any base wax you may have applied. Most wax manufacturers make small scrapers with portions contoured to fit the groove of the ski. It is important to remove old wax so that it does not build up in lumps on the ski or in the groove and promote icing. Many skiers never wax in the groove, and use a fast running paraffin there instead for fear of icing. This is foolish, however, as it represents a sizable proportion of the total surface area of the ski bottom.

If your skis ice up or a build-up of snow occurs on them, thus eliminating slide, always rewax rather than struggle on, hoping conditions will change. I have often sensed icing conditions such as these and found that by choosing the terrain carefully the snow build-up can be avoided. Wire fences and tree branches lying on the snow also make good wax scrapers. Simply slide back and forth on them. The edge of a plowed road or a snowmobile track also is effective for this purpose.

Figure 98   *Roller Skis*

7   CONDITIONING

Cross-country racing demands superb conditioning and a year round training program is essential to attain this. Even the recreational tour skier and bushwhacker will enjoy the sport far more, however, if he or she maintains at least a minimum level of fitness. While perfection of technique is what wins races, it certainly helps to develop strength and stamina as well. For this reason, one should develop practice procedures which assist both.

ON-SNOW TRAINING

Distance running is important if you expect to race, or simply ski, long distances. The first time I ran 30 km. in competition was certainly an eye-opener because it was significantly further than I had ever run all-out before. Things begin to happen as you pass the threshold of your experience, causing your technique to deteriorate further and increasing the physical strain on your body. In the Canadian Marathon, running over 60 km. each day, it is particularly essential to concentrate on technique. Here small things, such as blisters on your hands from pole swinging, can become annoying especially when you have never had this problem before. To avoid muscle cramps and other problems, it is essential to ski longer and longer distances gradually to train for events such as this.

To improve technique, ski with better skiers than yourself and follow or parallel their tracks closely, attempting to maintain their glide.

DRY LAND TRAINING

Before the skiing season begins, there are many exercises which will improve your physical condition and technique.

Running

This is of course an excellent all-year-round pastime and skiing for me is one way to keep up the activity during the winter.

Hill Running

Running up hills is a great way to build the stamina needed for racing. Use a pair of poles to aid balance and develop poling power as well. Here in Ontario, some of the fanatics tie weights on their poles and their boots to make it all a bit harder. If you live in a city, step running can be good training. Try climbing fifteen stories of the fire stairs in your apartment building, at a full run, half a dozen times, and you will begin to feel similar effects. Often the steps of a stadium or any grandiose public building are good because it is possible to run down as well. I do not recommend running down fire stairs as this often becomes a landing to landing leap which can result in injury.

Poling Exercises

These exercises which are done by using weights on ropes, are quite good although it is important to realize that the poles contribute, or should contribute, only a small portion of the skier's total forward power; therefore, becoming a muscle man in the arms and shoulders will really not make a better skier.

Roller Skis (see fig. 98)

These provide a good dry land training device as the diagonal stride can be reproduced nearly perfectly and poling can be as well if rubber tips are attached to the poles. In case you are wondering, these skis are fitted with ratchet devices which prevent the wheels from rolling backwards!

DIET

Cross-country skiing can burn calories at a phenomenal rate, sometimes well over 1,000 per hour in competition. Carbohydrate-high food will assist in maintaining the blood sugar level necessary to sustain this energy loss. During longer races, it is necessary to supplement the sugar loss while running. Warm tea laced with honey or dextrose-rich warm fruit drinks are excellent during a race, but one should be careful not to take too much. Moderation in eating just before a race is wise, especially foods with a high fat content and those that are difficult to digest.

On a ski tour, bring a lot of high energy food, such as chocolate, dates, and peanut butter. Bring oranges to provide liquid as they are far easier to carry than a canteen. Never eat snow, no matter how great the temptation. Allowing it to melt in one's mouth is safe, but swallowing ice can lead to severe and completely debilitating stomach cramps.

KEEPING WARM

Becoming cold while skiing can cause serious cramps and so carry the extra clothing required for any emergency. After a long tour or race, find a hot soaking bath or a sauna, drink a lot of liquid, and go to sleep.

Few feelings appeal more completely to my hedonistic nature than that of the perfect exhaustion after a long strenuous tour or race. Cross-country skiing permits uniform and gradual fatigue to overtake the entire body. Like swimming, it leaves hardly a muscle neglected.

GLOSSARY OF TERMS

Alpine Skiing   Downhill and slalom race events as well as downhill recreational skiing; as opposed to Nordic or cross-country skiing.

Anorak   Wind parka of lightweight material, usually with a hood, that is worn over sweaters or down parkas, etc.

Balaclava   Heavy wool knit cap which covers the entire head to the top of the shoulders with a face hole. Can be folded up and worn as a conventional tuque.

Base   Pine tar or pine tar derivative coating that is burned onto the bottoms of all wood skis before waxing.

Base Wax   Wax applied beneath the surface (or running) wax on the base to improve adhesion.

Bail   Clamping device which fits around the boot upper and presses down the sole over the pins of the normal pin binding.

Biathlon	A relay cross-country race and rifle shooting competition.
Back Slip	When the kicking foot in the diagonal stride slips back due to improper wax.
Binding	Device for fastening ski boot to ski, once called the "harness"
Basket	Ring at base of ski pole to prevent it from penetrating the snow excessively.
Camber	The bend built into all skis to make the pressure on the snow more uniform.
Combined	Nordic skiing event composed of the best performance in a 15 kilometer cross-country race and a 60 meter jumping competition.
Dubbin	Boot grease for waterproofing.
Edge	To angle one's skis into the hill to prevent them from slipping sideways down the fall line or to effect a turn.
Fall Line	A line directly down the hill, the shortest distance to the bottom.
Frostnip	Mild surface frostbite which occurs in areas of naturally poor circulation in the skin, such as earlobes, nostrils, etc.
Glissade	Sliding on one's feet and using a pole or poles for a brake. In mountaineering, an ice axe is used.
Glide	Amount of free slide which the skier obtains on his forward or riding ski during his stride.
Groove	Depression in the bottom of the ski to make it run straight and not wander left or right.
Grundvalla	A *base* material or pine tar derivative.
Grundvox	A base wax.

Heel	The tail or trailing edge of the ski.
Kick	Push of rear leg during the stride when the weight is being transferred totally to the gliding ski.
Lignostone	Compressed beechwood which has been impregnated with a phenolic compound. Used for edges of hickory ski bottoms.
Nordic	Cross-country racing events and jumping events. Recreational cross-country skiing as opposed to downhill skiing.
Orienteering	A sport combining map and compass reading skills with skiing or dry land running.
Pole Plant	Sticking the poles or a pole into the snow at a precise location and instant in time.
Pop-Up	A rubber or spring metal device fastened to the top of the ski under the heel of the boot to prevent ice and snow build up, it " pops up" when the heel is raised.
Pin Binding	A toe-only type binding having pins or studs which project into holes in the sole of the boot.
Relay	A team race where only one skier skis at a time, tagging another team member for his start of the next leg upon his own finish.
Running	Traveling on skis while utilizing the diagonal stride or other technique to maximize speed.
Shortening Clamp	A hinge device in a cable binding which clamps the cable tight by shortening its length. Used in the "Tempo" and "Kandahar" bindings.
Stride	A skier's sliding pace and the basic technique which enables him to progress efficiently.

Surface Wax   Running wax applied on the surface of the ski bottom which comes in direct contact with the snow.

Sole   The bottom of the ski.

Shell   A lightweight nylon parka.

Slip-Pass   When the trailing ski in the telemark turn slips behind the boot of the forward ski, causing one's legs to become crossed and an immediate and usually unavoidable fall.

Side Camber   The taper of the ski when seen from above. Wider in front than at the back so that the latter tends to track in a straight line behind the tip.

Tip   The leading point or front of the ski.

Tail   The trailing edge or rear of the ski, also called the "heel."

Tonkin Cane   A Chinese bamboo used for ski poles.

Traverse   To cross a slope away from the fall line while either ascending or descending.

Torch   A Propane, Butane, or gasoline blow torch used for "burning in" wax on the ski bottom.

Track   The trail left by skis in soft snow or a prepared racing trail. For the latter, the ski tracks are best seven inches apart on the inside.

"Track!"   The call of one skier to another when he wishes him to move aside and allow him to pass.

Tuque   A small cap for the head usually of wool and usually stretchable like a sock.

Telemark   A steered downhill turning maneuver requiring touring equipment.

APPENDIX

PLACES TO GO SKIING

The cross-country skier can find suitable terrain for skiing virtually anywhere, in the country and within the city, and so a listing of resorts is not really necessary. However, if you are just beginning and wish to rent equipment, have some instruction, or simply stay at a nice place in the country, I am including a listing of places which cater to cross-country skiers. It is wise to telephone, even if you are not interested in lodging or food, simply to verify the information contained here and to determine whether there is equipment available for rent, what the condition of the trails is, and whether snowmobiles are prohibited. Try to keep away from snowmobiles, if possible, because these machines ruin a ski track, not to mention spoiling the quiet of winter.

No list is ever complete. The following is no exception:

L-Lodging; T-Trails; I-Instruction; R-Rental Equipment.

In the East

Adirondack Lodge Heart Lake Lake Placid, New York	L,T
Blueberry Hill Farm Brandon, New Hampshire	T,R
Cross-Country Ski Place Wiscasset, Maine	T,R
Edson Hill Lodge Stowe, Vermont	L,T,R
Dana Place Inn Route 16 Jackson, New Hampshire	L,T
Northwood School Lake Placid, New York	T,I
The Wildcat Tavern Jackson, New Hampshire	L,T,I,R
The Trapp Family Lodge Stowe, Vermont	L,T,I,R
Tucker Hill Lodge Waitsfield, Vermont	L,T,R
Sugarbush Inn Warren, Vermont	L,T,R
Gray Ledges Grantham, N.H.	L,T,R
Okemo Mountain Ludlow, Vermont	T,R
Limberlost Lodge Highway 514 Huntsville, Ontario (705) 635-2251	L,T,R

Viking Ski Touring Center So. Londonderry, Vermont	T,R
Woody's Cracker Barrel So. Londonderry, Vermont (802) 824-5556	L,T,R
Skyline Ski Tour Lincoln Guide Service Lincoln, Mass. (617) 259-9771	T,I
Jay Barn Inn Route 242 Jay, Vermont 05859	L,T,I,R
Mountain Meadows Lodge U.S. Route #4 Killington, Vermont 05751	L,T,I,R
Eleven Thirty Corner Manchester Center Vermont 05255	L,T,I,R
Alp Horn Inn Chestertown, N.Y. 12817	L,T,I,R
Franconia Inn Route 116 Franconia, New Hampshire 03580	L,T,I,R
The Inn at Saw Mill Farm West Dover Vermont 05356	L,T,I,R
Woodstock Ski Touring Center Woodstock Country Club Woodstock, Vermont 05091	L,T,I,R

In the West

Yosemite Mountaineering School Yosemite National Park California	T,I,R
Vizzo Nordic Ski School Hope Valley, California	T,I,R

Ashcroft Ski Tours Aspen, Colorado	L,T,I,R
Scandinavian Lodge Steamboat Springs, Colorado	L,T,I,R
Beaver's Lodge Winter Park, Colorado	L,T,I,R

High Country Lodge   L,T,I,R
Mora, New Mexico

Trail Adventures   L,T,I,R
de Chama, New Mexico

Teton Village Resort   L,T,I,R
Jackson, Wyoming

Vail Resort Association   L,T,I,R
Vail, Colorado

Big Sky   L,T,I,R
Gallatin Gateway, Montana

West Village Association   L,T,I,R
Snowmoss, Colorado
Attention: Chuck Fothergills

Keystone Mountain   T,I,R
Dillon, Colorado

Crested Butte Ski Area   T,I,R
Crested Butte, Colorado

Sun Valley Nordic Ski
School   L,T,I,R
Sun Valley, Idaho 83353

Tourist Organizations Offering Mountain Touring Trips, Instruction, and Guide Service

1. Mountain Travel (USA) Inc.
   6201 Medau Place
   Oakland, California 94611
   (415) 339-8310

   Mr. Leo LeBon

2. Canadian Mountain Holidays
   132 Banff Avenue
   Box 583
   Banff, Alberta, Canada
   (403) 762-3709

   Mr. Hans Gmoser

3. Raids a Ski Bernezat/Puissant
   3 rue Pasteur
   Seyssins (Grenoble)
   France
   Mr. J. L. Bernezat

Write for Ski Touring Information:

In the East:
Ski Touring Council Inc.
342 Madison Avenue Rm 727
New York, New York 10017

In the West:
Far West Ski Association
812 Howard Street
San Francisco, California 94103

In between
Central Division
Ski Touring Council, Inc.
4437 First Avenue South
Minneapolis, Minnesota 55409

Figure 99   *The Author Finds Some Snow in Downtown Toronto*

PLACES TO GO RACING

Anyone living in the USA should write to:

The US Ski Association
US Ski Team Office
1726 Champa
Suite 300
Denver, Colorado 80202
Attention: Mr. Jim Balfanz, Nordic Program Director

Canadians should write to:

The Canadian Ski Association
Tower "A"
333 River Road
Ottawa, Ontario K1L 8B9
Attention: Mr. Irvin Servold, Chariman
Nordic Committee

Generally, most large races where touring classes are included are open to any individual without any restrictions, while strictly racing class events require USSA or CSA membership, club membership and sometimes a competitor's card.

The above national officers will direct the interested reader to his nearest divisional association, where he can become qualified to compete and obtain race calendars and other information.

Major Cross-Country Skiing and Touring Races

Most of these events have touring classes which are open to anyone who cares to pay the small entrance fee. Most are well organized and will provide contestants who register by mail with advice on accommodation which is available. All are a lot of fun.

The Canadian Marathon is run the last weekend in February each year over 90 miles of beautiful trails starting in the Laurentians, north of Montreal, and ending in the Gatineau Hills, outside Ottawa. This is a two day race with mass starts at 8:00 a.m. Saturday and Sunday. The course is divided into approximately 10 mile-long sections and tour racers are not permitted to start a new section after 2:00 p.m. In 1972, nearly 1000 competitors turned out, most of course only completing one or two sections each day. The course is well illustrated by detail maps and profiles of each section in a book that is provided for each registrant.

Write: The Canadian Ski Marathon
c/o Viking Ski Club
Box 57
Morin Heights, Quebec

Washington's Birthday Ski Touring Race is run over an approximately 15 kilometer course in the heart of Vermont's best touring country near the Putney School in Putney, Vermont. It is run on the Sunday closest to Washington's Birthday (February 22) and attracts many competitors.

Write: The Washington's Birthday Race Committee
c/o The Putney School
Putney, Vermont 05346

The Madonna Vasa covers 24 kilometers between Madonna Mountain in Jeffersonville, Vermont, and Underhill Center. It is held the first Sunday in March, the same day as the Vasaloppet in Sweden.

Write: Dr. John Bland
         Upper Valley Road
         Cambridge, Vermont 05444

The Stowe Derby is an annual 7 mile event usually run in February.

Write: Stowe Derby Race Committee
         c/o Stowe School
         Stowe, Vermont 05672

V-J-C Ski Touring Race is held outside Minneapolis in late February each year. Several hundred participants are normally expected.

Write: North Star Ski Touring Club
         4231 Oakdale Avenue
         Minneapolis, Minnesota 55416

The John Craig Memorial Ski Touring Race is held early in April over an 18 mile course used by the pioneer ski mailman.

Write: Oregon Nordic Club
         Bend
         Oregon 07701

Paul Revere Cup is a family and team event open to all held at Fort Devens in Ayer, Massachusetts in mid-February.

Write: Paul Revere Cup Race,
         P.O. Box 427, Concord
         Massachusetts, 01742.

Top-of-the-World Championships is a complete Nordic X-try competition held in the first half of April in Inuvik, North-West Territories. It is restricted to Divisional Teams by invitation only. Write to the Canadian Ski Association for complete information.

The Colorado Gold Rush Ski Race is a family type event covering around 12 kilometers near Breckenridge, Colorado, at 10,000 feet.

Write: Chamber of Commerce
             Frisco, Colorado 80433

The Estonian Open Ski Touring Race is a 20 kilometer event usually held on the first weekend in March in country near the site of the Muskoka Loppett in Ontario. Come to this one and you will see the best racers.

Write: The Estonian Ski Club
             301 Riverside Road
             Oakville, Ontario

The Muskoka Loppet is a 30 kilometer event through beautiful forests in the Muskoka Lakes region in Ontario. It is run on the second Sunday in January and attracts several hundred entrants.

Write: Muskoka Winter Association
             Box 1239
             Huntsville, Ontario, Canada

Jack Rabbit Family Ski Tour is an annual event run early in March over a 16 kilometer course in Southern Ontario.

Write: The Jack Rabbit Ski Club
             Attention: Neil MacDonald
             341 Dixon Park Crescent
             Mississauga, Ontario

SISU Races, run on the first weekend in February at the Finnish Ski Club in Udora, Ontario, attract top quality racers for 5, 10, 15, and 30 kilometer events. Enjoy a sauna and Finnish cooking, too.

Write: SISU Ski Club
             c/o Mr. Markku Rojala
             2200 Avenue Road, Apt. 601
             Toronto 380, Ontario

In addition, write to the US and Canadian Ski Associations for the current calendar of touring events. For the calendar of the very active Quebec/Laurentian Ski Racing and touring organizations, write to:

> The Laurentian Ski Zone
> 306 Youville Square
> Montreal 125, Quebec

> or, The Canadian Ski Association
> Quebec Division - Nordic Section
> 881 Maisonneuve Boulevard East
> Montreal 132, Quebec

International Classes of Competitors
As set by the F.I.S.
(Fédération Internationale de Ski)

MEN

Class	Age on January 1	Maximum Race Length
Senior	21 and over	F.I.S. - 50 km., otherwise unlimited
Senior	20	20 km.
Junior	18 and 19	15 km.
Younger Junior	16 and 17	10 km.
Older Boys	14 and 15	5 km.
Younger Boys	12 and 13	3 km.
Small Boys	11 and under	2 km.

WOMEN

Class	Age on January 1	Maximum Race Length
Senior	18 and over	F.I.S. - 10 km., otherwise 35 km. touring
Junior	16 and 17	5 km.
Older Girls	14 and 15	5 km.
Younger Girls	12 and 13	3 km.
Small Girls	11 and under	2 km.

North American class breakdowns are *not* consistent with the above. Many senior classes are differentiated into numerous veteran categories up to age 40 and over. Competition is extremely keen in the 30-40 year age groups and even older.

International Events
Courses are as prescribed by the F.I.S.,
(Fédération Internationale de Ski)

Course	Total Elevation Gain
5 km. women's	150-200 meters
10 km. women's	250-350 meters
10 km. men's	300-450 meters
15 km. men's	450-600 meters
30 km. men's	750-1000 meters
50 km. men's	1200-1500 meters

North American events often deviate from these standards. Courses in flat country, of course, do not have the elevation gain prescribed and others have far more than that prescribed.

In addition to the normal running events, relays, the biathalon, and the combined events are usually held in major competitions. These are as follows:

Relays
Three or four men run ten kilometers each and four women run five kilometers each. Courses are laid out with two parallel tracks and the race is an all-out sprint from start to finish.

The Biathalon
This is a twenty kilometer cross-country race with four men running five kilometer legs, each shooting at targets twice enroute. The racer carries a rifle and is scored for marksmanship as well as total team elapsed time.

The Combined
This is a fifteen kilometer running event combined with the sixty meter jumping competition, the winner having the highest placing in both events. It is an especially coveted event in Norway at the annual Holmenkollen competition. In 1968, an American, John Bower, won this event, a spectacular achievement.